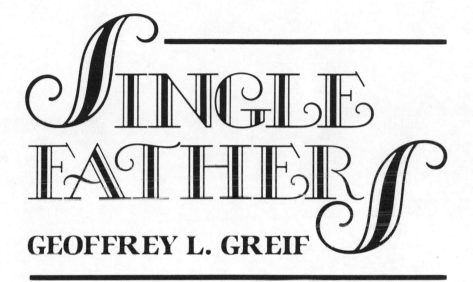

# SINGLE FATHERS

**GEOFFREY L. GREIF**

**Lexington Books**

*D.C. Heath and Company/Lexington, Massachusetts/Toronto*

*Library of Congress Cataloging in Publication Data*

Greif, Geoffrey L.
   Single fathers.

   Bibliography: p.
   Includes index.
   1. Single fathers—United States. 2. Fathers—United States. 3. Father and
child—United States. 4. Custody of children—United States. I. Title.
HQ759.915.G7     1985     306.8′56    84-48541
ISBN 0-669-09594-x (alk. paper)
ISBN 0-669-09595-8 (pbk. : alk. paper)

# Contents

# Tables

# Preface and Acknowledgments

This book began as a doctoral dissertation while I was attending the Columbia University School of Social Work in New York and commuting by train from my home in Philadelphia. During those days I became very familiar with that section of the rail system. The bulk of the book was rewritten in its current form in Philadelphia after I had finished school. Oddly enough, it was completed on another part of the rail system—the run from Philadelphia to Baltimore, where I have been teaching at the University of Maryland School of Social Work and Community Planning. I considered dedicating the book to Amtrak, but thought better of it.

I have been interested in men's issues (people's issues?) since the early 1970s. My master's thesis dealt with men's consciousness-raising groups. The study of single fathers came later, as an outgrowth of my continued interest in men's roles and of my sharing with my wife, Maureen, the child rearing of our oldest daughter, Jennifer.

A few points need to be made. This book deals primarily with single fathers because their story needs to be told. A research project on mothers without custody, an equally important side of the coin, is now being completed. As will be shown in this book, these mothers are an important and misunderstood population. What they experience at the hands of society is harmful both to them and to the fathers described here.

A number of tables, as well as a detailed description of the methodology and limitations of the study, appear in the appendix. This information has been provided for those wishing to know more about the study and the fathers who completed the questionnaire. All names and other identifying information have been changed to protect confidentiality.

Finally, I have tried to write the book so it will be useful to two audiences— those who study, work, and teach in fields that deal with family relations, and those who, though not professionally involved, have a personal interest in or curiosity about fathers raising children alone.

## Acknowledgments

There are many people to thank. The original study was funded by two foundations that wish to remain anonymous, but the people who make up these foundations should know I am eternally grateful to them for a number of reasons, the least of which has been the financial support they have given.

Ann Parks and Ginnie Nuta, at Parents Without Partners and *The Single Parent,* have aided me considerably since 1981. Lee Robeson, Hoyt Walbridge, and Jim Conroy have provided statistical support in dealing with the data. The students I have taught at the University of Maryland, Cabrini College, and Widener University have helped me by showing interest and enthusiasm along the way. As always, there was a great deal of typing and retyping. Rita Bell cheerfully accepted this task and made it more pleasant, as Essie Bailey had done with an earlier version. Brenda Frank needs to be thanked for her editorial comments, as does Carol Meyer for influencing a great deal of my thinking about social work and teaching.

Kathy Wasserman, who co-wrote chapter 11, displayed interviewing skills and insight into the children that made the chapter a pleasure to complete.

I have also been assisted on a variety of levels by the other researchers from whose work I have borrowed in writing this book. Wallerstein and Kelly's work has been particularly helpful. I hope I have given them all sufficient credit for influencing my thinking.

Perhaps most important, I have been helped by the single fathers who took part in the survey and the fathers whose homes I visited and whose children I interviewed. They were always willing to do whatever they could to assist me and to help other single fathers. Special thanks must be given to the family who were interviewed for chapter 2. Their openness made the work much easier.

Finally, to the three people who help me to be a father—Maureen, Jennifer, and Alissa—this book is dedicated. (Did I have a choice? No, there was no other choice!)

# 1
# Introduction

Allen came home one day and found that his wife had run off with one of his friends. He was left with the house and two children. Allen had known things were shaky in the marriage, but he had not expected this. Suddenly he was left with a number of brewing crises. He had to decide what to tell the children. He had to go to work and arrange for child care. He had to figure out how to do the housework, handle the laundry, and prepare meals. Finally, he had to sort things out for himself. There were many things about his failed marriage he did not understand. Three months later, Allen's wife returned. Her new relationship had fallen apart, and she wanted the children and the house. Allen said no, and they went to court. The judge thought the children were better off staying where they were: Allen won.

Mario and his wife had not been getting along for years but had stayed together for financial reasons. When Mario was passed over for a promotion, relations between them deteriorated. They started fighting more and more. Sometimes the children would get involved in their fights. Mario had become more involved in parenting because his wife was spending time away from the house, job hunting. The morning after a particularly bad fight, they decided to split up. They both wanted the children. Mario wanted them because he loved them and believed he could raise them alone; however, he agreed to move out, and his wife took over the responsibility. A few months later, when she became unhappy with the situation, she moved out, and Mario moved back into the house with the children. He has been raising them alone ever since.

Frank and his wife had slowly grown apart during their ten years of marriage. They had married when they were both young and still in college. His wife thought she had given up a lot to be a wife and mother. Now that their child was older, she felt less needed at home. She wanted to be something other than a housewife. Frank was settled in a decent-paying job, and she was looking for employment. When they split up, letting Frank raise their child seemed the natural decision. He had a more stable income and more regular work hours, and she would be better able to find work if she was not strapped with child care.

This book is about single fathers who are raising children following the breakup of their marriages—fathers whose situations very nearly fit those of

Allen, Mario, or Frank, and other fathers whose experiences are very different. What they all have in common is that they are raising children without the children's mother living in their home. (Widowers have been excluded because of the focus here on the continuing relationship with the noncustodial mothers.) These fathers are living a nontraditional life-style that is rare but becoming increasingly common. Not much is known about these men. Yet how they manage raising their children has far-reaching implications for our view of fathers and mothers.

The roles of fathers and mothers, men and women, are a mirror of our lives. Our reactions to people who occupy nontraditional roles say as much about us as about the people we are observing. What we think about fathers with custody is an indication of how far we have come in understanding ourselves. It is the contention of this book that we do not know enough about fathers who have custody. We form conclusions about them that are often incorrect. We base assumptions about them on information—often fallacious—that we get from movies, books, newspaper articles, television, and our own views of the way men and women should behave. We construct myths about these fathers.

Because of these myths, we take a dichotomous view of the single father that, by implication, is restraining and demeaning to both fathers and mothers. This dichotomous view is built on two assumptions. On the one hand, we assume the father is an extraordinary man simply because he is raising his children. On the other, we assume he needs our help with cooking, cleaning, and child rearing because he had not had much experience with those chores.

The first assumption is an outgrowth of our heritage. Throughout most of the twentieth century, mothers have been the primary caretakers of children. They have taken care of the children in the home and have run households. They have been the nurturers. In the words of Talcott Parsons, they have fulfilled an "expressive" function. The fathers, fulfilling an "instrumental" function, have served as the guide to the outside world.[1] They have worked in that world and have supported the family financially. They have negotiated for the family with the world and educated the children about how to be successful when they leave home. More recently, however, with mothers entering the work force and more men taking part in housework, this concept, formed in the 1950s, has become obsolete. The roles of the mother and the father do not fit neatly into Parsons's framework.[2] We see men in greater numbers than ever before changing diapers, taking their children to the park, and generally nurturing them. Yet the obsolescence of the Parsonian conceptualization should not be seen as proof that there is now equality in our expectations of the sexes. There is not. Even though mothers work outside the house, they are not as well represented in the work force as men are. The man is still the primary and, in many cases, the sole wage earner. In only 11 percent of working couples does the woman earn a higher income than the man.[3] According to the Census Bureau, women entering the work force earn less than men entering it.[4] At home, by contrast, the mother is still the executive. Although fathers are doing more around the house, in terms of both housework and child rearing, many of these duties are not shared equally. The mother still carries the major responsibility. Yes, there has been a sexual revolution, but, no, there has not been a *coup d'etat*. Men and women are still carrying out fundamentally traditional behavior.

When a father has custody, people assume he is an extraordinary man. They think he must be incredibly dedicated to his children, and they believe his children must be dedicated to him. They wonder how he can do all the things he has to do: work, run the house, cook, take care of the children. Socially, he is often seen as a good catch, especially to the single mother, because he is good father material.

At the same time, dichotomously, he is seen as someone who needs help. How can he know how to cook, clean, and shop for clothes for his children? How can he know how to discuss sexuality with an adolescent daughter? People feel sorry for him and run to his aid. They feel sorry for his children. They offer him assistance in the form of recipes and lectures on hair braiding. They say to him in the same breath, "You're great," and "Let me help you."

These reactions to single fathers are based on myth and on tradition. The goal of this book is to discuss what 1,136 fathers have gone through in raising their children. By learning how these men handle the demands of single parenthood, we can gain a more accurate picture of single fathers, of single mothers both with and without custody, and of role expectations for men and women. These men are in a crucible. Because they are on the fringe of society, they provide a way for us to look at how role expectations are carried out, how men get along without role models, and how we feel about fathers doing what mothers have traditionally done.

## The Single-Father Phenomenon

In 1983 there were almost 600,000 divorced and separated single fathers raising children under eighteen years old—an increase of 180 percent since 1970. During the same period, the percentage of divorced and separated single mothers increased by slightly over 105 percent, to 4,256,000.[5] By 1983 these fathers were raising almost 1 million children,[6] a number that continues to grow. Many theorists believe both the number and the percentage of single fathers will continue to climb during the 1980s. There has also been a sharp rise in joint custodial arrangements. Although the statistics on sole custodians can be documented, the statistics on parents who are sharing custody cannot. The Census Bureau has no category for fathers or mothers who have their children on weekends or half the time. A parent is categorized as either having children in the home or not. As a result, no one is sure to what extent joint custodial arrangements have become more common, although clearly their growth has been significant.

What we are seeing is part of a trend toward greater involvement by fathers in both divorced and intact families. The increase in men's involvement in parenting roles has been attributed to a number of factors. The first of these is the women's movement. Starting in the early 1960s, and inspired in part by the civil rights movement and the publication of books on feminism by Germaine Greer, Betty Friedan, and others, the movement and its proponents have sought equality in every facet of American life. The impact of the women's movement has been felt in the workplace, the armed forces, elective and appointed political offices, and our personal lives. Both Sandra Day O'Connor and Geraldine Ferraro represent political choices made by men seeking women's votes. In the home, the women's movement has contributed to greater paternal involvement to fill the vacuum left by women entering the work force. For children, this has meant having less contact with their mothers, spending more time in alternative child-care situations, perhaps being left alone. Sometimes, too, it has meant more time with their fathers.

The women's movement as an isolated factor has not caused these changes, however. Since the early 1960s those adults who are now parents have witnessed many changes—a popular musical revolution; the growth of a middle-class drug culture; great affluence and technological advances; and political disillusionment brought on by the assassination of John F. Kennedy, the Vietnam War, and the Watergate scandal. In this context, the women's movement can be seen as one of many important factors that helped pave the way for profound changes in the life-style of many Americans.

The upshot of these changes is that men and women have more options for behavior than ever before. Women have increased job opportunities. In 1970 only 37 percent of children under eighteen had a mother in the work force. In 1984 that figure had increased to over 50 percent.[7] Because of these changes, women are better able to define themselves in nonmaternal ways; they can be successful at something other than motherhood. Fathers also have more options. Men have joined consciousness-raising groups; have become househusbands; and have become more involved in the diapering, feeding, and bathing of babies. Whether or not these changes for men and women are short-lived and will be reversed remains to be seen. For now, the result has been increased avenues for individual expression and fulfillment.

With these changes have come others as well. There is a greater blurring of sex roles. Men have more leisure time. With their wives working, they can work shorter hours and still have the family's income remain stable. With increased free time, men can become more involved with their families.

There is also a subtle change in the way men view themselves. We have become a more open society, more willing to examine our feelings. Many men have thought about their own childhood and concluded they missed something when they were growing up because their father either was not home as a result of a demanding work schedule, or was distant when he was home. Fathers want to give their children a different experience, and they want a different parenting experience for themselves than their own fathers had. This is part of the makeup of what has sometimes been described as the new man, the softer male who is less macho. He reportedly understands women and their needs. He is interested in a sharing relationship with a woman that is not constrained by traditional roles.

This new man image that has emerged in the last ten years can be found portrayed in television shows and the movies. A look at the Academy Awards over the past several years shows that the new man as actor or as a theme has been consistently winning the Oscars. The following table shows the winners in two key categories since 1977. An asterisk indicates the winner that reflects this new trend. Prior to 1977, awards usually went to movies that expressed other themes or to actors who embodied a macho image.

|  | *Best Movie* | *Best Actor* |
|---|---|---|
| 1977 | *Annie Hall* with Woody Allen in his typical nonmacho role | *Richard Dreyfuss as good father material in *Goodbye Girl.* |
| 1978 | [*The Deer Hunter*] | *John Voight plays a soft, warm Vietnam veteran in *Coming Home.* |
| 1979 | *Kramer vs. Kramer* | *Dustin Hoffman immortalizes single fathering. [Robert DeNiro] |
| 1980 | *Ordinary People,* where father and son find each other. | |
| 1981 | [*Chariots of Fire*] | *Henry Fonda as grandfather working out issues with daughter and grandson. |
| 1982 | *Gandhi* for the man and the epic film | *Ben Kingsley as Gandhi. |
| 1983 | [*Terms of Endearment*] | *Robert Duvall as a drunken soft-hearted father in *Tender Mercies.* |

Whether this trend continues remains to be seen. But certainly these awards reflect a shift in the images we have of men.

The second reason for the increase in paternal involvement is the high divorce rate—a phenomenon that has been linked to the first reason, the women's movement. Between 1970 and 1982 the rate of divorce rose from 47 divorced persons per 1,000 married persons to 114 per 1,000.[8] Although the divorce rate leveled off in 1982 for the first time in many years, the high rate of divorce means there are still numerous opportunities for men to be sole parents. With every divorce involving children, there is a chance that a father will become the sole custodian of his children. Many fathers do not want to lose their family. They are willing to go to great lengths to get custody because their children are vitally important to them.

The third reason for greater involvement in single parenting by fathers has to do with the legal changes that have evolved because of the women's movement and other social changes. Fathers now have a better chance of gaining custody in court in disputed cases. Yet although fathers' chances are clearly better, there is a heated debate between feminists and fathers' rights groups as to whether there is equality between the sexes when there is a court battle. Feminists claim the father now has the upper hand; fathers' groups argue that mothers are still favored. To understand the nature of this battle, a brief history of custody decisions is needed.

## Custody in Perspective

Prior to the twentieth century, a father was much more likely than a mother to be a single parent raising children alone, for two reasons. First, the high maternal mortality rate plunged many fathers, especially in rural areas, into widowhood.[9] Second, fathers had social status, whereas mothers—and women in general—had none. Mothers were rarely granted custody in cases of divorce because they had little chance of supporting themselves independently. Women who had worked on the farm or at home, once separated from their husband, had no salable skill or property that could produce enough income to support a family. Children were also seen as second-class citizens, essentially the property of their fathers.[10] The mother's status was so much lower than the father's that even when the mother did have custody, the courts usually absolved the father of paying child support.[11]

By the late nineteenth century, a number of humanitarian organizations such as the Children's Aid Societies, welfare bureaus, and the Charity Organization Societies, working in a climate of progressivism, helped to change the legal position of children. The notion that the child was the property of the father was slowly replaced with the view that the child had rights of his or her own. The mother's role also changed as an outgrowth of the Industrial Revolution. With the transformation from an agrarian society in which all family members worked together to an industrialized one in which the father worked outside the home, the mother increasingly had to stay home to take care of the children. This generated a change in the view of the mother's importance.[12]

The early years of the twentieth century were accompanied by continued industrialization and urbanization that further pulled families away from the farm. With these shifts in population, with the growing suffragist movement, and later with the support of Freud, the mother's role came to be further respected as vital during the child's so-called tender years between birth and four, when the mother was the person most responsible for the child in an industrialized society.[13] Bowlby's work on maternal deprivation in the 1940s and 1950s further bolstered this idea of the mother's importance to the child.[14]

The changing view of the mother's role in child rearing affected the way the courts made their decisions when custody was disputed. The bias toward the mother during the middle fifty years of this century was such that the only way the father could obtain custody was to prove her unfit.[15]

This bias toward the mother remained intact until a few years ago, when, with the women's movement and other social changes, sex role expectations began to change. At present there is spirited debate over whether fathers and mothers have achieved parity in disputed court cases. Polikoff (1982) and Woods, Been, and Schulman (1982) claim that men now have the upper hand in court because judges are using economic criteria to decide who is most fit. In such a contest, the father has the advantage. Atkinson found, after a review of appellate court cases in 1982, that fathers and mothers were roughly equal in the number of contested cases won. He concluded that mothers may still hold the edge in the number of trial court cases won.[16] Regardless of who holds the edge, these decisions should be made in a sex-neutral fashion (see Polikoff 1984).

A cursory look at custody cases that have been reported in the *Family Law Reporter* (1982), which covers recent court decisions, shows great variation on the matter. Two cases exemplify this. In a Missouri court in 1982, the court found, ". . . if both parents are employed and equally absent from the home, the mother has no more part in training, nurturing, and helping in the child's development; and if everything is equal, the mother has no better claim to child custody." Here the issue of equality is soundly upheld.

A few months later, however, in Virginia, the state supreme court found in favor of the mother even though there were good reasons to give custody to the father: "Given the 'tender years presumption' in favor of mothers, the fact that a mother's third suicide attempt resulted in hospitalization and continuing psychiatric care does not deprive her of her superior custody rights against a father whom the court finds to be an 'excellent parent.'" From these cases one can see that the way a father or mother fares in court can be totally idiosyncratic to the state, the county, the judge who tries the case, and also the parents and their lawyers. This great variation makes it difficult to draw conclusions about whether either party holds the upper hand in disputed custody cases. It is clear, however, that the father's position has improved greatly during the last decade.[17]

These three areas of change—the women's movement along with the other social factors cited, the high divorce rate, and greater equality for men in court—are all responsible for increased involvement by fathers in parenting and for more single fathers gaining custody following separation and divorce.

## The Survey

Despite the increase in the population of single fathers, we have very little information about them. A few small studies have used sample sizes of less than 100 drawn from one section of the country. The purpose of the research that underpins this book was to gather needed descriptive information about these fathers and to examine how comfortable and satisfied they felt meeting the tasks of single parenting. A number of variables were used to explore the impact of different factors on the father's experiences.

The study was carried out by placing a four-page questionnaire in the May 1982 issue of *The Single Parent*, a magazine published by Parents Without Partners (PWP). PWP, founded in 1957, is the largest self-help group for single parents in the United States. Any custodial or noncustodial parent—whether single, divorced, widowed, or never married—may become a member. At the time the survey was published, PWP's membership was slightly over 200,000. It is estimated that about one-third of that membership is male.

Divorced and separated fathers who were raising at least one child eighteen years old or younger for a majority of the time were invited to return the questionnaire that appeared in the magazine. Questionnaires that made up the final sample of 1,136 fathers were received between May and August 1982. At that point a data set was established, and questionnaires received after that time were set aside.

The fathers who made up the final sample had sole custody at least twenty nights a month or more. Fathers with joint or shared custody, or those whose children spent half their time somewhere else, were excluded from the survey. It was believed that such fathers would not have to make the same types of adjustment that fathers who had custody a majority of the time would have to make. For example, a father whose child's mother is readily available might not have to deal with such issues as a daughter's sexuality. Such matters could be left to the child's mother. Although many fathers with joint custody do handle these issues themselves, the possible variability could not be handled easily within the confines of this study. The father with primary responsibility for the child must either handle these matters himself or arrange to have a relative, teacher, friend, or other adult do so. Either way, this would require more work on the father's part.

Since the publication of the questionnaire, more than 100 personal and telephone interviews have been conducted (primarily with fathers living on the East Coast near the author) in order to bring a greater understanding to the information gained from the survey. These interviews, which were completed in October 1984, along with the questionnaire results, form the basis of this book. What we are hearing then is the father's story. (For a further discussion of the survey, its methodology, and limitations, see the appendix.)

### The Fathers in the Study

The fathers who completed the questionnaire varied greatly in terms of age, occupation, education, income, and the number of years they had been raising their children alone. There were fathers as young as twenty-two and as old as sixty-five. There were fathers who were factory workers and laborers and those who were lawyers and doctors. A number of men had not completed high school, whereas others had doctoral degrees. Their incomes ranged from less than $10,000 to over $100,000. Some men had had custody for over fifteen years; others had had their children for less than one year. Almost all the fathers were white, and most were either Protestant or Catholic.

The fathers were raising 1,996 children eighteen years old and younger. Derdeyn (1976b) has written that fathers are more likely to get custody of their children if those children are boys and if they are not of "tender years." Among these fathers, some support is given to this contention. There was a greater tendency for the child being raised by the father to be a boy than a girl (57 percent were boys). The average age of the children being raised was between eleven and twelve. A father was nearly as likely to be raising one child (39 percent had one child) as two children (43 percent had two), with the rest of the fathers raising anywhere from three to six children alone.

### When Children Are Split Up

In some situations, the father raises one child and the mother another child. This arrangement can come about for a number of reasons. There may be different alliances between parents and children. If one parent has to move away because of work or a new relationship, one child may decide to go with that parent while another may want to stay in the home town. One parent may be more financially stable. Approximately one in five single fathers had children eighteen and under living somewhere else, usually with the mother. In further support of Derdeyn's contention concerning which parent is more likely to be raising certain children, 63 percent of the children being raised elsewhere were girls. There was also a greater percentage of children four years old and younger—8.4 percent versus 5.8 percent—being raised elsewhere than with the father. The reason for the difference in the sex and age of the children being raised by the father from those of the children elsewhere is that the tender-years presumption may have influenced the father not to seek custody of younger children or of girls, just as it may have influenced the mother to keep these children, and the judge to favor the mother as the sole custodian.

A profile of the average father in this study shows a man forty years old, employed in a middle-management position, who has completed two years of college and earns $28,000 a year. The average income for all single fathers, including widowers and never-married fathers, was $21,000 at the time of the study.[18] A word needs to be said about the differences in income between the fathers in this study and the average income of all single fathers in the United States.

One common assumption put forth by others who have studied single fathers who are raising their children is that these fathers usually come from middle- or upper-middle-class backgrounds. It has been stated that fathers with more education and higher incomes are more likely to have come from liberal backgrounds and more apt to feel financially and emotionally capable of raising their children.[19] It may be true that fathers with higher incomes are better able to wage a court battle and that judges see them as more fit. Because of the lack of available data, there is no way to know whether divorced and separated fathers, rather than widowed or never-married fathers, do come from higher socioeconomic classes. In black and Hispanic families, however, which tend to be matriarchal in structure and have a lower average income than white families, it is less common for a mother voluntarily to relinquish custody of her children. This means that the single fathers in the United States raising children following separation and divorce may be of a higher socioeconomic class than *all* single fathers, including widowers, never-married fathers, and single fathers from lower economic classes.

The typical father in the survey has had sole responsibility for his children for 3.5 years, about the same number of years he has been single. This indicates that most of the fathers gained sole custody at the time of the marital breakup or shortly thereafter. The typical father also was married for about twelve years before the breakup and gave his marital status as divorced.

Many of the men in the study were born in the 1940s. This means they were brought up in an age when roles were traditionally defined. They were usually married in the 1960s, before or at the beginning of many recent social changes. Hence these men may have relatively old-fashioned views of the way men and women should behave, which would affect how they adapt to being single and how they handle some of the demands of parenthood.

Although a typical profile has been drawn of the fathers in the study, it is important to remember that there is great variation among the fathers. A profile gives only a general view of the population. Learning about each father and his experiences broadens our understanding of all the fathers.

## About This Book

This book will describe how fathers handle the various aspects of parenting—housework and child care, going to a job while raising the children alone, socializing, getting along with their children and ex-wives, and dealing with the legal system. Mostly, it is the father's story being told as he discusses what his life is like raising his children alone. Other views are offered in the chapters on children and single mothers, but this is a story that must be told from the father's perspective. It is *his* story, and not much is known about him. At the same time it must be remembered we are hearing only his side of the story. With such an approach there is often bias.

These fathers are not extraordinary men simply because they have their children. In many cases they have become single fathers not so much because of their participation in housework and child care during the marriage, but because their wife abdicated the role she had been fulfilling. These men change when they become single parents, but they still to some degree retain their typically male stiff-upper-lip mentality.

The chapters of this book are organized in a way that follows the father from the time his marriage is in trouble, past the custody decision, and through the different demands of single parenting. Chapter 3 discusses the marriage, divorce, and custody decision. Chapters 4 through 9 examine the father's experiences as he takes care of the housekeeping and child care, balances the demands of work with those of parenting, establishes a relationship with his children, attempts to begin a social life, deals with his ex-wife, and maneuvers his way through the legal system. A number of variables were hypothesized to have an impact on the experiences of the single father in his attempts to raise the children. These variables were the age, sex, and number of children the father was raising; his income; the number of years the father has had custody; the involvement of the ex-wife with the children; and whether the father wanted custody. These variables will be discussed in each chapter as they apply.

A study conducted a year later of 150 mothers with custody who completed the same questionnaire as the fathers is included in this book as chapter 10. It provides some basis for comparison between what fathers and mothers experience raising children alone.

Finally, two chapters have been included that were based solely on interviews. One chapter deals with some of the experiences of children being raised by single fathers. The other, which is chapter 2, is composed of interviews with one family who went through the experience of being headed by a single father many years ago. Adult children, now in their twenties, talk about what it was like to have grown up with their father as their sole guardian, and how they view marriage and their parents now. This chapter sets the stage for much that follows.

It is important to make clear the perspectives I used when viewing the findings. A number of perspectives were involved as no single one was adequate.[20] One was a feminist perspective that views women as victims of sexism.[21] Clearly, as stated before, I see men as being victims, too. In the later chapters when I talk about how men and women are perceived and the differences between them, it is not meant to condone the inequities between the sexes, but to describe them. One goal of this book is to reduce those inequities.

Second, the life cycle perspective had its influence. In this perspective, all families are seen as having "crisis" periods that are a normal part of life.

These periods occur when there are role and developmental changes in the family.[22] The oldest child graduating from high school, the negotiation that goes with doing the housework, and adjusting to new work demands are all normal events in a family. Many of the conflicts the fathers in this study experience are not the sole province of single-parent families.

Third, the literature on role ambiguity has been important. Single parents are often caught between worlds where the expectations for their behavior are not clear.[23] The theory here has provided me a framework for understanding this.

The literature on coping and adaptation has helped me organize my thinking.[24] Many of the chapters in this book deal with the tasks of parenting. These require a coping response if they are to be handled successfully. The fathers who have mastered these tasks feel more competent about themselves as parents.

Finally, I have looked at the information from a systems framework. What this means is that everyone in the family has an influence on the other family members. The children and the father are simultaneously dealing with the absence of the mother and the establishment of a new family.[25] The mother without custody, regardless of the amount of contact she has with the children, has an impact on them, as do the school, the father's job, friends, and relatives. In turn, the father and the children affect all of these people. Within this context it is difficult to consider the father as an isolated person. The attempt has been made to discuss those other people that influence the father's experiences. The reader is invited to join me in applying these perspectives when trying to understand the father and his family.

A final note to the reader: The term *custody* is used throughout the book to refer to the situation in which a father is raising children alone. Not all fathers officially have custody. They have not necessarily gone through a legal process. They may informally have custody of the children because of an agreement, either stated or unstated, with their ex-wives. For the sake of simplicity, however, *custody* is used loosely in this book. It applies to all situations in which fathers are raising children after separation and divorce. (It must also be noted that this book is not meant to be an up-to-date description of the legal issues surrounding custody decisions. Impressions about the legal system are offered but the topic is handled in much greater depth by others.[26])

By the time the reader has finished this book, she or he should have a better understanding of this growing population, and the myths people hold about single fathers raising children alone should finally have been laid to rest.

# 2
# Twenty Years Later: The
# Story of One Family

This chapter is the story of one family, taken from interviews with a
father and the four children he raised. Unlike all the other families
discussed in this book, where there are children eighteen years old or
younger, this father gained custody of his children almost twenty years ago.
The children, now adults, talk about their experiences growing up as well as
their current feelings about marriage, relationships, and child rearing. They
also candidly discuss the differences between being raised by their father and
by their mother. The father gives his impressions of his failed marriage, how
he gained custody, and what life was like for him raising four children when
single fathers were much rarer than now.

The interviews with the family members took place in June and July 1984.
Four of the five family members were personally interviewed, and the fifth was
interviewed by telephone and through written correspondence. The three sons
were interviewed together. The family members could talk off the record if they
wanted to give the author specific background information about a situation
without having the information included in the chapter. The mother was ap-
proached but refused to be interviewed. When Susan, the oldest child, found
out her mother had refused to take part in the interviews, she told me: "I knew
Mom wouldn't agree to talk to you. I'm sorry for you because she is so neat. But
Mom's basic feeling is that it wouldn't help us kids, so why bother? I hope you
can understand that instinct in her. It's very basic to who she is."

Trying to weave five people's lives into a coherent story has proved difficult. There are different impressions of major family events. Harsh, angry
feelings are expressed, as well as warm, happy ones. Their stories aptly illustrate how one family grew up. As such, they provide a framework for
understanding the families currently being raised by a father. At the time of
the interview, the youngest child, Keith, had just graduated from college,
signaling an end to the parents' responsibility for their children. It was a fit-
ting time to ask the family to reflect on growing up with a single father.

## The Family

Peter and Gail, both fiftyish, are the father and mother. Peter runs an art
gallery. Gail is a newspaper reporter, an occupation she has held since 1953,

when they were married. The children are Susan, now twenty-eight; Barry, twenty-six; Vince, twenty-five; and Keith, twenty-three. The four children live in three different cities; two of the children live near their mother, and none lives near Peter. The three oldest are successfully employed in a variety of professions; Keith is just entering the job market. At the time of this writing, both Susan and Vince, who are married, report serious problems in their relationships, and both are either going through a trial separation or actively seeking a divorce.

### The Family before the Divorce, the Divorce Itself, and Custody

One thing that Peter said attracted him to Gail was that she was "pretty sexy." There was also an "opposites" attraction. He saw Gail as being spontaneous and very lively, while viewing himself as sober and somewhat reserved. Both of them worked at the beginning of the marriage. Gail would take time off from work with the birth of each child but, because of the nature of her work as a reporter, was able to return to work on a part-time basis very soon afterward. After their last child, Keith, was born, she returned to work full time. A housekeeper was hired to take care of the children and the home. The family lived near a major eastern city.

According to Peter, as Gail became more successful in her work, she began spending more and more time away from home in pursuit of stories. Sometimes she had to do her interviews at night. Peter felt the housework and child care were falling increasingly on him. He resented the extra responsibility and resented the fact that she was not home much with him or the children. Her investment in her work rather than in the home and the marriage became one of a number of major stumbling blocks in the marriage. In the last year they were together, tempers flared. During one particularly bad fight, Peter says, he hit Gail for the first and only time in the marriage. Gail ran crying into a back room of the house and shut the door. Shortly thereafter, Peter and Gail separated, and she took the children.

(As will be seen throughout this chapter, Peter's memories can be quite different from those of the children. Children sometimes forget certain events and may overdramatize the particulars of others. This can also be true for adults.)

The three sons, who were between four and eight when their parents split up, do not remember much about life with both parents. The two oldest boys do recall their parents fighting occasionally and the hitting incident just described. They report that their father was always accusing their mother of not fulfilling her motherly duties and that one time, during a fight, she scratched his face after he accused her of having an affair. When Peter left the house for his own apartment, Barry, then eight, was told by Gail that the reason for the breakup was that his parents did not love each other anymore. Vince, who was one year younger, was told that he was too young to know. Looking back, the three sons are still unsure of the reason for the divorce. They have suspicions about what was going on but no clear idea. Susan also does not know of any specific reason. She does remember her parents constantly reassuring the children that although they did not love each other, they both loved them.

During the year they lived with their mother, their old house was sold and they moved to a smaller home. Peter used to see the children on the weekends. He found being a noncustodial father hard, even though he was on good terms with Gail. He says: "Basically, she was a very good mother and we agreed on most things. Everything was done amicably. I had not really considered taking the children. I stayed very involved with the children. But I found it difficult to have to plan weekends, and she resented my spending time at their house, so I had to take the children away from there. It was a problem to spend time with them and it was a problem to entertain them." During this period, Peter says he was making weekly support payments. By all accounts, Peter was a very involved noncustodial parent.

### Why Peter Gained Custody

Not only do the memories of adults and children differ, so too do the stories given by divorced spouses as to what has happened. In this situation, Peter is speaking for himself; the children are relating what they remember and also what they heard from Gail.

After living with Gail for a year, Peter gained custody of the children. The reasons for this vary depending on who is telling the story. Peter says that Gail was having a hard time handling the children, especially the three boys. She went to a lawyer to get help in giving custody to Peter for a year, at which point she wanted to get the children back again. Peter agreed to take the children but said he would not give them back after a year. He felt having the children shuffle from house to house was not in their best interests. Peter said he was happy to gain custody of the children, although he had never really given much thought to what it entailed. It had never occurred to him to pursue custody actively before Gail relinquished it, although Peter remembers wanting the children because he was unhappy with the way the housekeepers Gail hired took care of them.

The children have a different version of what happened during the time they were living with their mother. Although they do not recall many details of their living situation, the sons believe they went to live with their father because he was not making support payments and their mother could not afford to raise them.

Susan, after speaking with Gail, also gives a different account from that given by her father. She says her father was not paying child support and that he took custody of the children in part because he was about to remarry and Gail thought two parents were better than one, and in part because he was unhappy with the way they were being raised. Financial problems brought on by Peter's lack of consistent support payments were also plaguing Gail. Susan adds that after Peter had custody for a year, he wanted to give the children back to Gail, who refused, saying it would not be good for the children to go back and forth.

The children do not recall anything traumatic about the actual switch from one house to the next. They say that one day their parents told them to pack their things to go live with dad. Susan says: "It occurs to me how flexible we all were. I don't remember being sad at the move. I've always been close to dad and I was thrilled to be back in the city [where he lived]." At the time, the children were between four and nine years old. Looking back on that time, Susan says: "I do know how much pain she went through having to give up her babies. Mom used to do wonderful things like rock us to sleep, all four of us stretched out on her bed. And she used to wake us up in the morning with a special song that we still remember. It was incredible to me how much energy she put into mothering us."

## Life with Dad

The first thing Peter says he did when he got custody was to hire a housekeeper. She became the first of a stream of housekeepers who were to play an important part in how the children were raised until Keith reached high school. Peter says that having someone there was a big help to him. The children remember spending a great deal of time with housekeepers. When they were young, this meant that neither the children nor Peter had to deal with the drudgery of housework, which would become a major bone of contention when the children were older.

### Money

Money was a recurring problem for the family. During that time, Peter's art gallery business was up and down, which meant the family's income also fluctuated. The lack of consistent income over the years left the children with the impression that life was full of great financial uncertainty. According to Peter, Gail would buy them clothes and toys but never sent child-support payments to Peter. The children remember her giving them all the things that their dad could not afford. When Peter's business was going well, there would be a celebratory mood in the home, followed by periods of belt-tightening.

Other memories concerning money stand out for the children. Vince remembers seeing his father crying one day because of problems with his business. Barry and Keith remember that when things were bad financially, their father's temper flared more quickly. Vince said, looking back on that time: "Finances really put the screws to Dad. Mom did not feel financial pressures and he did, so he screamed more."

*Social Life*

All the children were popular when growing up. They never felt singled out because they were being raised by a single father. In fact, they said many people did not seem to know they were living with their father. When teachers mentioned a special project that the children were supposed to work on with their mothers, the children made a mental adjustment to asking their father for help or would go to Gail, who, by the children's account, remained very involved with them.

Many of their friends were also products of single-parent families, and this may have eased the transition for them. Vince felt there must have been some common bond that attracted him to the children in these families.

The family moved many times during those years but always stayed in the same school district, so the children's friends remained the same. The reason for the frequent moves was that they lived in rentals because Peter could not afford to buy a house. The constancy of the neighborhood was calculated by Peter to make it easier for the children.

There were bittersweet experiences, also. The children sometimes felt more appreciated by their friends' parents than by their own. Barry and Vince were good athletes; after sporting events, which the children remember Peter as rarely attending, the boys would get a great deal of attention at their friends' houses but little at their own. This attention helped to sustain them but made them resentful of their own situation.

A different set of circumstances also drove them to friends' homes. The boys in particular remember there never being much food in the house, especially the kind of junk food children thrive on. They would go to their friends homes for all the goodies they could not find in their own cupboards.

As already discussed, the memories of children and parents often differ. So do the perspectives they bring to situations that arise. What the children understood about Peter's need to socialize comes from a child's perspective. Adults see these needs in another light. To the children, Peter's dating took him away from them; to Peter it was a necessity.

Peter's social life was very active. Peter explained to the children that they would have to understand his need to socialize and that his life could not totally revolve around them. Peter says there was rivalry at times between the women he dated and his children, but he never felt his social life was handicapped by being a single parent. Some women were turned off by his having children; others were drawn to him because his parenthood made him a more attractive potential husband.

During the time the children were growing up, Peter remembers spending occasional nights out with women. Women were more likely to spend the night with him, usually coming after the children were asleep and leaving early in the morning before they woke up. Peter did not feel the children were bothered too much by his dating.

The children, however, remember being upset by their father's dating. Susan says: "I was jealous of the women Dad dated. And I think they were jealous of the relationship he had with me." Barry remembers being put to bed and then seeing Peter leave. Vince once walked in on Peter when he and a date were lounging in bed. Vince thought nothing of it at the time. All the children feel their father was a better parent when he was not dating because then he had more time for them.

One year after Peter began raising the children, he married a woman named Lisa whom he had been dating for a while. Peter had reservations about the marriage, thinking she did not fully understand what she was letting herself in for with four children, but she pushed for it. She made no real attempt to parent the children after she moved in. One reason she did not try was that she was small, and most of the children were physically as big as she was. Another is that she did not have what Peter describes as a "maternal instinct"—a characteristic that Peter points out was notably lacking in all of his wives.

One year later the marriage ended. Peter says Lisa asked for a divorce because she was frustrated with him. Vince and Barry remember Lisa's leaving. She came out to the porch where they were sitting and started to cry. She told them she was leaving, that she loved them, but that she just could not live with their father. She has had no contact with the family since then.

## Housekeeping

Sometimes children in one-parent families are called on to do more around the home than they did when both parents were in the home. In this family, as in many others, the assumption of new responsibilities for Peter and the children led to problems. At times an oldest daughter is singled out as the father's confidant.

As the children got older, they began taking care of themselves with the help of Susan and Barry. A housekeeper was no longer needed. Peter says the decision not to continue to hire one was based on three factors: (1) the children's age, (2) the expense, and (3) the difficulty in getting a good housekeeper.

Without a housekeeper, the work that had been done by someone else fell on the shoulders of Peter and the four children. Sometimes Peter would be traveling and would leave the children on their own. Keith describes an evening routine of Peter being out, Susan cooking, and Barry going around and locking up the doors and windows. In addition to the housework, which the children shared with Peter, at early ages they made their own lunches, much to the amazement of their friends.

Susan felt that although she did the same amount of housework as the other children, she shouldered more of the emotional burden in the home. She said she played the role of the wife every day when Peter came home. She would ask him how his day had gone and talk with him about his relationships and the family's financial situation. This began when she was fourteen. This was also the age at which she ran away from home. "I was frustrated. I was feeling pressure at home from all the emotional responsibility. I ran away for a few days and then came back home. Dad never said anything about my being gone. It was like, 'Well, you've been gone and now you are back.' But even then, whenever we kids did something like that, we would call our mother and check in with her."

Without a housekeeper, the door was also open to a long series of battles over housework. The children state that their father would come home from work and say, "I work all day and should not have to come home and clean this house, too." The children say that Peter would resent Barry and Vince going to sports team practices because it meant they could not help out with the cleaning. They recall constant battling and screaming over the housework and being hit occasionally if it was not done. They feel they were given too much responsibility at the time and, in turn, not enough restrictions on their behavior. They were allowed to come and go as they pleased when they were growing up—a situation that made them, by their own description, "viciously independent."

Peter agrees that housework was a problem for the family. He feels he made a particular point of not putting too much pressure on Susan to take care of the younger boys. He wonders if he should have put more pressure on them to assume responsibility. He says he was home a good deal of the time and, if he had to travel, it was for no more than a week at a time.

The children recall one time in particular when he was away for a few nights and left $20.00 on the table for them to use for food. A big fight erupted over how the money should be spent.

*Father-Children Relationship*

A theme discussed in chapters 6 and 11 and repeated here is the difference in the nature of the relationship that sometimes develops between fathers and sons and fathers and daughters. The three sons differ from Susan in the feelings they hold toward Peter. In turn, the way the sons feel about Gail is also different than what Susan feels.

Vince and Keith said they were afraid of their father's temper. Keith said: "When things were bad, he was on us. We caught it. He slapped us a lot. He was unpredictable and would explode. But he would calm down immediately and everything would be O.K. right after that." Vince felt Peter picked on him especially: "He never gave us support. He deals with us now better as friends then he did when we were growing up. One time when he was picking on me a lot, I was twelve at the time, I decided to run away. Keith came too, and we rode our bicycles twenty-five miles to Mom's house. Only she wasn't home that weekend. So we stayed there alone." While Vince and Keith were upset and scared by Peter's yelling, Barry was able to immunize himself against it: "I did not let it bother me at all. I learned to ignore it."

Keith reported that after his siblings had grown up and left the house, his relationship with his father hit a particularly bad period. He remembers Peter being after him to do the housework and their having a fight during which Keith threatened Peter with a screwdriver. Keith said that after that point he got along much better with his father.

Vince believes Peter may have felt uncomfortable in his role as father. There were times when they felt he did not know what to do with them, and this made things awkward for everyone. Barry remembers his father sitting down with him to discuss sex: "I had learned all about it from the kids in school, and when Dad sat down with me to discuss it, I said I knew about it already. He seemed very relieved."

Susan reports a much different relationship with her father: "I've always been very close to my dad. Mom says it has been that way since I was born. Dad and I have some very similar outlooks on life. I've always made a special time to be with him and felt a lot of love from him. He was very involved in my life. We shared many of the same interests. I remember times in my life when I was hurting and he was there. But I also see that his relationship to me, as both parent and a person, was very different than the relationships he had with my brothers. They are much more angry."

The children feel that Peter's work was his salvation. It was what saved him from having to spend too much time at home in a role in which they feel he ultimately was uncomfortable.

Peter says that although he did find single parenting harder than he had anticipated, he enjoyed it. He realizes there were difficult times between him and the children, especially his sons. He says he had definite ideas about how things should be done around the home and admits to having a temper. His temper may have affected how well he got along with the children as they were growing up. He feels he spent an adequate amount of time with his children, however, given the circumstances of his work, and remembers attending many school functions in which they were involved.

When the three oldest children had left home for college, Peter married Helen, his third wife. Peter and Helen are currently separated. She did not play an important part in their upbringing but now, since she and Peter have separated, remains in contact with most of the children. She even attended Keith's college graduation. Like Gail and Lisa, Helen is described as having few motherly attributes.

Whereas the children saw Peter as begging for his freedom from them, he saw himself as trying in many different ways to get along with the four children while also trying to run a tight ship. There were many happy times, too. Both the children and Peter have fond memories of meals around the dinner table, and of trips to the beach. They did then and still do find Peter a fascinating person to talk with. Even though Peter did not have a fondness for sports in common with his sons, ("They must have gotten their athletic ability from their mother," he jokes), the sons tell of having an especially good time building things with Peter at home. Working on a project with their father took on a special importance for them because it was something they could all share in.

## Gail and the Children

The three sons took a protective stance concerning their mother. This was also true of the children interviewed in chapter 11.

During the time the children were living with Peter, Gail, according to the children, was playing a very important part in their lives. Not only were they visiting her an average of once a week, but she was giving them a great deal of emotional support. Vince said that Gail, who lived in a series of apartments, always picked a place to live where there would be an extra room to sleep in and a swimming pool or a basketball court nearby. Barry said that even though she did not live with them, he always knew she would be there if they needed her. "We knew we were a priority in her life," he said. Keith said: "She was there when we felt lonely, sad, or beaten up on. We could call her." Susan adds that their mother was the key parent for her brothers, whereas her father was the key parent for her.

Susan's relationship with her mother when the children were younger was different: "I was the only person who really rejected Mom. My brothers, especially Vince and Barry, never did that. Sometimes I think this is also the reason Dad felt so comfortable with me. I think I really felt deserted by her. But I also saw to it that we did not speak. There was about a year and a half when I refused to have anything to do with her. She'd call and I wouldn't talk to her if I answered the phone. So you see, in a way, Dad had me all to himself. And I was pleased as peaches to be the apple of his eye."

As Susan grew up, their relationship changed. "It's easier for me to discuss my relationship with Mom as it is now. When I turned nineteen it was as if there was this sudden desire to get to know and understand this lady, and we've been very close ever since. As I've gotten older it is now Mom who I turn to for emotional guidance and assistance. We talk at least once a week. We share some crazy times laughing. It's been just a joy for us to grow closer and closer."

Sometimes if there were fights in the house and Keith was feeling overwhelmed by his older siblings, he would call Gail and she would mediate over the phone, talking first to one child and then to the other. Peter, out shopping for art, was often unreachable at those times. It was also Gail who attended sports events at school and gave support where the sons felt Peter offered very little. Occasionally she would come to school conferences, too.

Although the children loved the attention they got when they went to their mother's (she would cook special meals for them and buy them clothes), they also were aware that she was spoiling them. Like their father, she did not put many restrictions on them. Vince perhaps depended on her the most. During his junior and senior years in high school, he spoke with her on the phone every day. He would call her each morning to wake her up for work: "If I did not call her, she would get up late."

The children are happy their parents have stayed on such good terms. They feel they reaped the benefits. For seven years after the breakup the whole family continued to get together for Christmas. Gail and Peter, along with Peter's third wife, Helen, attended Keith's college graduation. As well as they got along, the children are aware that things are better than if they stayed together. "They are such opposites," Keith says. "I would rather have the family we have now where everyone gets along. We have the best of both worlds. They made a good team, but I am glad they did not stay together. They did not love each other, and it worked out better for all of us."

Peter has a different view of the relationship between Gail and the children. He does not think she was a very involved parent: "She would see them on the weekends, but I always thought she was breezing in and out and trying to fit them into her life. She never offered to take them for any length of time. One time I called her and said: 'Look, I have to get away for a vacation for a week. Would you please take them?' She was happy to do it but she never offered on her own. She almost never made any attempt to regain custody of them." Because of what he perceived as her lack of concern about the children, he seldom consulted her about decisions affecting them and handled them on his own.

## Now

The children, having described their experiences growing up, were asked to talk about how they see their lives now. They were asked about their views on being raised by their father, marriage, and having children. They were also questioned about their apparent protectiveness toward their mother.

The sons, for different reasons, feel sorry for both their parents. They feel their mother, who never remarried, sacrificed everything for them. They see her as the victim in the relationship between her and their father. It is this perception of her as a victim that may cause them to be protective of her now. There is no such protectiveness evident when they talk about their father.

They feel sorry for their father because of the awkwardness they think he felt as a father and because they think he now feels guilty about not spending more time with them when they were younger.

Susan has no such feelings of remorse for either parent, but she is more content with her own situation. (One of the more interesting points that came out of the interviews is that, despite some of the anger the sons in particular feel for their father, both they and Susan are glad they lived with him rather than with Gail.)

The children were asked to reflect on whether they felt there was anything different about being raised by a father than by a mother and whether this had any effect on them now as adults. This is a difficult issue because the way that one is parented is idiosyncratic to the personalities of the father and mother and to other facets of the home situation. Also complicating this question is the fact that the children were not isolated from their mother while they were growing up.

Vince said that one of the differences in being raised by a father was that they turned out to be stronger people, more independent: "We grew up faster."[1] Keith states: "We all benefited from living with him. Mothers are so damn protective. We were exposed to things that a lot of kids were not exposed to. We were better off without her, but we knew she was on call. Dad either taught us or forced us to have responsibility. We are all very commonsensical. From our first bicycle on, we have learned how to raise money and go out and do our own things so we can survive, and we have gained a lot from that which could be due directly or indirectly to Dad."

One exchange between the sons further brought out some of the issues they were feeling about being raised by their father and not their mother, and the impact it had on them. Barry said: "Glad we weren't raised by her. She would have spoiled us. It was nice to go there and be spoiled, but it turned out better being raised by Dad." Keith responded to this, "I don't know if we had lived there full time if she would have spoiled us." Vince added: "She didn't really have the chance to spoil us. She had us three months out of twenty-five years."

Barry looked at his brothers for a moment and said: "We are all viciously independent. With relationships, I have had a hard time. I am very selfish because I am used to getting my own way, because we always got our way. There was no one to tell us otherwise." Vince agreed with this: "Yeah, we all have built cubicles around ourselves, whether it be for protection or because we've had to. Almost to the point of being selfish like Dad. Because we have had so little, we are reluctant to relinquish what we have. So we're selfish."

"Do I wish Mom raised me instead of Dad? This is a funny question," Susan wrote, "and one that I have talked a lot about over the years. Mom would have been a lot stricter with me than Dad. Dad basically gave me free rein. But I was never in need of a lot of supervision and restrictions. I don't know how I would have turned out with Mom. I know when it comes to the custody issue, I wouldn't break up my children, but I would agree to let my husband raise them if he could do a better job of it. But I have this very keen desire to have children one day."

Susan, in a separate conversation, echoed this theme of independence: "I'm probably more independent and self-sufficient because of all of the love I have gotten from him." She adds that it has had a positive effect on her relationships with other people: "An interesting thing has resulted from the [pending] divorce [between Susan and her husband]. I place such a strong emphasis on honesty and friendship from men, I've never really learned how to play games. Some men find this disarming. Men and I are equals and allowed to have the same or more similar roles in a relationship. This has caused a problem sometimes."

The sons also hold a view of women that reflects a great deal of respect for their equality. Keith says: "I see them as equal but think our peers do not. They have had two-parent families and have seen mothers in a certain way, and I think we see them in a more up-to-date way than they do." Vince, who is currently separated from his wife, agrees that women should be equal but admits to trying to get out of sharing the housework in his own marriage.

Vince wonders whether seeing his father always acting so protectively of his own feelings has affected his relationship with his wife. He finds it difficult to share his time with her in a way that may be similar to the difficulty Peter had in sharing with them. Keith reiterates the feelings of Barry and Vince but adds a dimension that is similar to that mentioned by many children of divorce: "We never had parents who showed affection for each other so it's hard to know how to do it now. I also feel there is this box that I have built around me. It is like the song 'Cat's Cradle,' where the father sees his son has grown up just like him and does not want to see him. It scares me to think I will be selfish like him. Kids like to be held and told they are loved and stuff like that."

Barry, hearing this reference to the song, said: "I am scared I am going to grow up like him, being selfish with my own children. I don't want to have kids." Keith also worries about how he will react with his children and wonders when he will be ready for child rearing: "What scares me is that I have seen so many families so neat and tight and think that is great. I don't have anything to give me guidelines. But I am hoping some day. . . ." Vince, because he is married, has given the most consideration to parenting. He feels good about the prospect of being a father: "I want to take my kids and do the opposite of what I got." Not having felt much support from his father, he wants to make sure his children get it from him.

Susan is the most optimistic about marriage: "Marriage is very important to me. Inside me I have this very basic belief that life is fair, and that even though this [marriage] did not work out, the next one will and I am not afraid to push forward."

Peter has been affected by his relationships with his children over the years. Not only has he become a lot more relaxed with them, he has moved increasingly into the role of friend rather than parent. He has become a lot more affectionate physically. Vince notes: "He recently has been very demonstrative and has done hugging and kissing in the last few years. For a long time there was no contact, but there is now. It makes me feel better. I like it." Peter believes he has done as good a job raising his children as was possible, and he is proud of them.

The children also talk about how well they have all turned out. Vince says how he is happily puzzled that, with all they went through, none of them got in trouble with the law or became involved with drugs. He and his siblings all echoed the belief that the family, despite various problems, has turned out well.

Susan, ever the optimist, said: "I only feel blessed for the relationships I have with both of my parents. They were always there when I needed them in very different periods of my life. And now that I'm away, our relationships have even gotten stronger."

## Conclusions

The family is now in a period of transition. The last child has finished college, and both parents can let go of a little more of their parenting responsibilities. The children now describe relations with their parents ranging from tolerant to very warm. Their personal lives reflect some failure and concern about future relationships. The sons worry about their ability to have adequate relationships with women. Yet they take pride in having turned out well. Their fears about how they will handle the future are on their mind, but at the same time they believe in themselves.

As will be seen, this family does not fit neatly into some of the categories described in later chapters. The family is rare, perhaps even among single-father families, in a number of ways. The mother stayed very involved with the children throughout their childhood. They had the opportunity to grow up knowing both parents intimately. The family also is rare in that housekeepers played a major part in maintaining the home. When the housekeepers were no longer around, some of the routine difficulties of cleaning had to be faced, and arguments began.

In other ways the family's situation is similar to that of many of the single fathers who took part in the survey. The family's fluctuating income was a recurring problem. Housekeepers could be afforded, but other amenities often could not. Peter's work schedule sometimes made family routines difficult to follow. As in many single-parent families, the children may have "grown up a little faster" because of the responsibility they all had. They became "viciously independent," perhaps at too early an age.

There is a general consensus among the children that being raised by a father fostered this independence, that mothers protect children more and spoil them. Their father had a more analytical or commonsensical approach that is a reflection of the way many men approach situations. In this sense, what these children had growing up is different than if they had been raised by their mother. What they will teach their own children, if they have them, will probably be different, too. Barry, Vince, and Keith want their children to have a better experience than they had. Susan hopes she can have as good a relationship with her children as she has with her parents.

For Peter and the children, as probably with all families, there is ambivalence and questioning about the past and the experiences they had. This is coupled with a good deal of confidence in themselves. In many ways, this family may represent what the experiences of the other families in this book will be in the future.

# 3

# The Study Results: The Family Before the Divorce, the Reasons for the Divorce, and the Reasons for Custody

**B**eing part of a family can be like taking a roller coaster ride. There are ups and downs, stops and starts, twists and turns, and periods of great momentum, all of which one can try to predict by studying the track or looking around the next curve. But the vagaries of the course nonetheless surprise, thrill, and sometimes scare the rider. When two people first consider each other seriously as future spouses, they begin the climb up the ramp to get on the roller coaster. If they are wise, they first study the structure, look at the person operating the ride, and wonder whether it is a safe one. When they get married, the ride starts. Traveling with them are all their dreams and expectations about the future, their past experiences, and their present day-to-day lives. Their friends are there, along with their families and their work worlds. The curves of the ride are sometimes easy and sometimes treacherous. Many couples stop the ride before they make it once around the track.

When children enter the family, the roller coaster ride takes on more momentum. The turns become more treacherous, the thrills more exhilarating, the stops and starts scarier. Many families can hang together and make the ride fun. Other families cannot make it and decide to jump off.

Usually, when families jump off the roller coaster, the children live with their mother, and the father becomes the visiting parent. For the fathers in this study, however, something different happened somewhere along the route. At some point, the mother and father took on unconventional roles, and the father ended up with custody. A father receives custody as the culmination of a number of different events that occur at various points in time. There is no specific single characteristic that these fathers and mothers possessed during their marriage or at the time of their breakup that would have predicted the outcome. There is no one event that can be singled out as the reason the father is raising his children.

The pictures drawn of fathers with custody vary greatly. Even so, some trends do emerge that characterize the different periods in the father's life preceding custody. These periods of time will be observed separately, and the common elements of these fathers' experiences will be detailed. These periods of time include the marriage; the time when things were going well (if they ever were) and the period when things were not going well; the breakup; and the time during which the custody decision was made. From those time periods, profiles of different custody situations can be drawn.

## During the Marriage

Interviews with the fathers concerning their parents' marriages, their own experiences growing up, and the first year of marriage seldom revealed anything noteworthy. Some fathers had come from intact families, others from single-parent homes. No trend was found among the fathers in their religious upbringing or the importance placed in their own families of origin on keeping a family together. Thus there was no common element at the start of the marriage among these fathers that could point either to their marriage failing or to their gaining custody.

The research reviewed on the single father's role in the family during his marriage tends to describe the father as being fairly typical in his involvement with the children. Gersick (1979), for example, found no difference between custodial and noncustodial fathers in their degree of participation in child rearing during the marriage.

The fathers in this study were asked to indicate their level of involvement during the marriage in the areas of housekeeping, child rearing, and breadwinning, as compared with their wives. The findings support the notion that these fathers were not living radical life-styles during the marriage, although they may have been more involved than the average father in some areas of child rearing. The vast majority of the housekeeping—usually a traditionally female function, with the arguable exception of the shopping—was handled by the wife. The child-care involvement was more often shared equally, according to the father, or was handled primarily by the father, indicating greater involvement on the part of fathers in this area. The breadwinning role, a usual male bastion, was primarily the fathers' responsibility.

Although the fathers in the study, *by their own description*, seem to have participated in child rearing, many of the fathers interviewed did not perceive themselves as being very different from the average father during the good period of the marriage. It is important here to draw a division in the marriage between the good period and the transitional period leading up to the divorce. During the early part of the marriage—the good period—the division of labor in the marriage was apt to follow more traditional lines. The fathers used words like *average* and *normal* when asked to compare themselves with other fathers they knew at the time of their marriage. Jeff, a mechanic, was one such father: "We started off like everybody else. I worked and she did the home. When the kids came, she took care of them. I was doing as much at home as the next guy. Later, when she changed, I started doing more."

Two difficulties arise in asking fathers to compare themselves with other fathers. Some fathers are members of peer groups who clearly do more around the house than most men do in the United States. Chang and Deinard (1982) suggest fathers with custody tend to have a higher income than fathers without custody. Comparisons with those groups do not accurately reflect the extent of the father's involvement compared with other fathers who are not in his peer group. Another difficulty is that the impressions given by the father can be inaccurate. One father of three from Minnesota, who felt he was very involved with his children, learned that his daughter had a different impression. He said: "I was president of an athletic association which my kids and my wife were involved in. I was president of the recreation program. That took a lot of time. We spent a lot of hours and money planning and improving the parks in the city. After the divorce, my daughter came to me and said, 'I know you did this and I know you did that, but when we had a problem you did not have time.' But they never really came to me and said, 'I have a problem.' They saw I was busy and went to Mom instead."

Other fathers in the study definitely were more involved than was typical with their children and with housekeeping during the marriage. One father said: "I was more involved than most during the marriage. So it was easy for me. I did a lot of cooking, so it was not a big change when I had to do it all the time. She was working at a job where she did not get home until later than me, so I cooked. I had to do the shopping and some of the cleaning." This is similar to the story told by Peter, the father in the previous chapter.

Another father, whose involvement began at the birth of his child, shared most of the child care with his wife: "We took the birthing classes together, and I was there when our son was born. I stayed involved. It was part of who I was. I used to give him baths, feed him, and change him." This father is one of the ones who described himself as having "average" involvement compared with other fathers, yet he was doing more around the house than most men do. What can be concluded from this discussion is that most of the fathers, while the marriage was good, were typical of all married fathers in their involvement with the housekeeping and child care. During the good period of the marriage, the father's relationship with his wife also appeared to be typical.

The fathers described a range of relationships with their ex-wives. Some fathers had very good, storybook relationships in which both partners shared interests while maintaining their own identity. Other fathers reported that their relationship was in trouble from the start but that they continued in the marriage, hoping things would improve. Jan was one such father. He sensed something was wrong with his relationship with his wife almost from the beginning. For religious reasons, after their children were born, they stayed together. When their youngest child was three, Jan learned that his wife was a lesbian. They stayed together for three more years, again for religious reasons.

Finally, after he slept with a prostitute and "learned what life was really all about," he asked her for a divorce. During the marriage, he had left most of the housekeeping and child rearing to his wife.

## When Things Turned Bad

In many marriages there comes a time when both partners realize things are not going as well as they had wished. Some of the fathers interviewed said they became more involved with their children because of a shift that occurred during the marriage. This is why it is necessary to distinguish between the good and bad periods. The shift that led to greater involvement came in three forms: either a shift in the father's impression of how his wife was parenting, a shift in the marital relationship that had nothing to do with the father's impression of the mother's parenting, or a shift in both areas. The father's response to those shifts followed five broad patterns. Although they had not been overly involved with the children during the early part of the marriage, the majority reacted by becoming more involved with the children when they perceived a change in their relationship with their mother or in her parenting. Two reasons were given for this: (1) to take care of the children, if the man thought there was a lack of nurturing on the part of the mother, and (2) to preserve a sense of family for themselves.

The fathers who became increasingly involved with their children because of a change in the mother's nurturing (the first pattern) were more apt to be fathers who were disturbed by their wives' behavior. For example, one salesman with two sons said: "She started to go out on her own and spend more time away from the family. She would go out with friends. I took over some of the things she had been doing that weren't getting done with the kids and with the house. Then she said she wanted a divorce." Another father said: "She had a number of mental breakdowns and would be away from the family in the hospital. Her mother moved in for a while and helped out. But I ended up eventually doing most of it."

These fathers were "forced" to become more involved with their children by their impression that the children's basic needs were not being met. It was the mother's withdrawal from the parenting role that got them more involved.

A second group of fathers became more involved with their children in an attempt to preserve something for themselves. They saw their wives' parenting changing, and either felt a great affinity with their children that they wanted to maintain, or had a need to maintain some sense of family. One father of two boys, who was a psychologist, was asked at what point he took over the major responsibility for his children. He said: "Two years before she left, we talked about the need for a separation. I felt she was off in her own world. I thought the kids should be with their mother. I was away from them for two days and I could not take being without them. So I came back and said if anyone has to leave it will have to be you. I don't know how I would have survived being a weekend parent. I knew this [having custody] was what I wanted, and she made it easier by being the one to leave." There were also fathers in this group who became more involved because they did not want to be alone or have another man raise their children.

A third pattern was found among some fathers who, even though they sensed a change in the marriage and an abdication of the mothering role by their wife, did not respond by getting more involved with the children. Men in this category candidly described turning to work as solace from an unhappy marriage or not getting involved because they were not "into" the children at that point in their own lives.

The fourth group of fathers saw the wife become more involved with the children as the marriage turned bad and responded by increasing their own involvement with the children. These fathers were competing for the children with the mother, fearing they would lose both. These four patterns describe changes based partly or wholly on a change in the mother's parenting.

Finally, a fifth group of fathers sensed a shift in the marital relationship that bore no relationship to the mother's parenting of the children. They perceived the mother as still fulfilling her parenting role even though the husband-wife relation was souring. Fathers in these failing marriages followed one of three paths: (1) They turned away from their children and their wives; (2) they maintained their previous level of involvement with their children; or (3) they increased their involvement with the children as they felt the marriage slipping away.

Thus there were five different groups of fathers with distinct experiences with the mother during the marriage:

1. Fathers who sensed a lack of involvement in parenting by the mother and responded by wanting more involvement with the children to fulfill the children's needs.
2. Fathers who sensed the mother's withdrawal and became more involved with the children to fulfill their own needs.
3. Fathers who turned away from the family when their wife also turned away.
4. Fathers who turned toward their children as the wife increased her involvement.
5. Fathers whose involvement had nothing to do with the wife's parenting behavior, but more to do with the failing marital relationship.

This discussion is meant to shed light on the majority of the predivorce households. In the usual course of events, the father and mother fulfill traditional roles as long as the marriage is going well. Some fathers, sensing a change in the wife's parenting, may become more involved with the children, eventually setting the stage for becoming the sole custodian.

## The Period of Divorce

Divorce is considered one of the most stressful life events. Nothing else breaks up a family in quite the same way—pitting one spouse against the other, changing the financial situation drastically, and leaving deep emotional scars. The period up to the divorce and the period immediately following it have been called the most stressful times. As one *New York Times* reporter wrote, "Divorce can exact a greater, and in many cases longer-lasting, emotional and physical toll on the former spouses than virtually any other life stress, including widowhood."[1] New life-styles have to be established, new friends made, explanations given. When children are involved, the problems are compounded. The adjustments to be made are greater, the feelings more extreme, and the emotional scars more difficult to handle, regardless of the age of the children.

The divorce itself was not anticipated by many of the fathers in the study: 44 percent said it was a surprise, 45 percent said it had been expected, and 11 percent were unsure. An even higher percentage, 66 percent, did not initiate the breakup, whereas 22 percent said they did initiate it, and 12 percent said it was a mutual decision. Of further interest, 58 percent of the fathers said they did not want the marriage to end, 30 percent wanted it to end, and 12 percent were unsure. These figures support other findings indicating that women are more apt to end the marriage than men are.[2]

These figures show that the mother ends the marriage more often than the father does and that the father is often unhappy about it. Perhaps that is why 73 percent of the fathers said the breakup was very stressful for them, and another 18 percent said it resulted in some stress.

The results give us new insight into these fathers. They do not tend to be special in their feelings about the marriage ending. They are as reluctant to have it end as are fathers who do not have custody. This further indicates that they were typical fathers during their marriage. As discussed earlier, they probably were not living radical life-styles in which the housework was shared.

Perhaps most important, it shows the men to be people who often are reacting to their circumstances rather than acting on them. Many had not actively sought greater involvement with their children during the marriage. In most cases, the father did not end the marriage. If they had, perhaps the resulting custody situation would have been more predictable.

## Reasons for the Divorce

The fathers in this study gave a wide range of reasons for the divorce—reasons similar to those given in other studies of single fathers. Their answers were in response to a question asking the fathers to describe, in their own words, the reason or reasons for the divorce. Their answers were grouped into the four general categories that occurred the most frequently.

### Shared Reasons

Three hundred eighteen fathers (28 percent) gave answers indicating that they and their wives shared the reason for the divorce, that it was a natural outgrowth of their relationship. This response did not assign blame for the breakup. Reasons that were placed in this category were "incompatibility," "communication problems," "sexual problems," "we grew apart," and "we fell out of love."

### The Wife's Infidelity

Two hundred seventy-six fathers (24 percent) responded that the wife's affair with one other person or a number of other people caused the breakup. This response often was accompanied by a good deal of anger about her unfaithfulness. (Only 12 fathers indicated that *they* were having an affair that caused the divorce.)

### The Wife's Leaving

Two hundred fifty-seven fathers (23 percent) reported that their wives left the marriage without implying infidelity on the wife's part. Reasons placed in this category were, "she fell out of love," "she wanted her freedom," "she wanted to pursue a career," "she deserted the family," "she wanted to find herself," and "she wanted to be single again." With this response, many of the fathers seemed to blame themselves. One father wrote, "I couldn't make her happy, so she left." Reasons given in this category were occasionally coupled with those from the shared category and the next category.

### The Wife's Problems

One hundred seventy fathers (15 percent) responded that their wife had some personal problems that caused the marriage to end. Examples were: "she was an unfit mother," "she was an alcoholic," "she was on drugs," "she was crazy," "she abused the children," "she could not cope with the children." Here the fault was placed with the wife.

These reasons can be seen as a way of predicting other outcomes for the fathers. The fathers who give shared reasons for the divorce tend to be the best adjusted to the demands of single parenthood. They also tend to have the most involvement with the ex-wife. There are many reasons for this. If the father feels the breakup of the marriage was due to both his own behavior and his wife's, he will not adopt either of the common extreme positions associated with divorce—blaming only the other partner or blaming only himself. The recognition and acknowledgment that a failed marriage is often the culmination of a dance both partners have choreographed and performed together can go a long way toward helping a divorced person to adjust. A man who reports that he and his wife could not communicate, or that they were incompatible, is not necessarily blaming any one person. Accepting part of the responsibility for the breakup reduces some of the acrimony divorced fathers often feel toward their ex-wives.

At the other end of the continuum were those fathers who blamed their ex-wives' infidelity for the breakup. These fathers seemed to have the hardest time dealing with the demands of parenting and the most difficulty adjusting to being single again. These are the men who feel the most hurt and anger; they feel wronged by their ex-wives. These men distrust women when it comes to dating again; they tend to be wary of getting hurt. Their anger toward their ex-wives also makes visitation difficult. It is difficult for a man to negotiate a visitation schedule when he feels his wife lied to him during the marriage.

The other two groups of fathers—those whose wives left and those whose wives had problems that ended the marriage—fall somewhere in between. Fathers whose marriages ended because of their wives' problems reported the least involvement with the children on the part of those women. In some cases the father blocked visitation because he felt his ex-wife was unfit. In other cases the mother absented herself from visitation because she felt insecure and ashamed of her problems.

The stories these men tell about the breakup of their marriages help us to understand the roads they traveled to reach their present situations. Their reasons for marital estrangement range from the story of the father who left to avoid his wife's violence to that of the man who said he and his wife still loved each other but just could not get along.

John, who was living alone at the time of the interview but also lives with his parents when he cannot make ends meet is raising a four-year-old son. He said: "The last few months [of the marriage] were hell. I was the main parent. We just started fighting and she would get violent with me and my daughter. When she got violent, I wouldn't retaliate." He wrote on his questionnaire: "Wife wasn't in full control of mental faculties and refused to seek appropriate help. History of these problems in her two previous marriages." Despite what John said in the interview, it was his wife who ended the marriage. He wanted to stay married and work things out, but she finally left.

Dwayne also did not want his marriage to end and was surprised when it did. He vacillates between sharing the blame for the divorce and blaming her alone: "It was partly my fault and partly hers. Our relationship became strained. Divorce is very debilitating financially and emotionally. I was sued and in court for months. I felt like the injured party. I came home one day and she was gone. She had been a vocal women's libber and made things strained." Dwayne wrote on his questionnaire, "Wife wanted new identity . . . was very involved with women's liberation movement." He is not discouraged about future involvements, though. To a question concerning how to get along better with one's children, he responded, "Get remarried, if possible."

Problems in Marty's marriage began with his wife's infidelity. He received custody of his five children in 1969: "My wife liked to run. I told her, 'If that's what you want, you leave the children with me and go.' The first years of the marriage had been good. Then something drew us apart and we went separate ways. I stayed home and let her go. She went first. We tried talking about it but sometimes I did not want to and sometimes she did not want to. No, we did not go for counseling." She initiated the breakup; he said he was unsure if he wanted the marriage to end. On the questionnaire he offered a variety of reasons: "Not mature. Lack of communication. Another man."

Al was another man whose marriage ended because of his wife's infidelity: "My marriage ending was a complete surprise. [Al wrote on the questionnaire that his wife had run off with another man.] In the last stages of the marriage she was contradicting me with the parenting, with my authority. That caused friction. We did not go for counseling. I never knew what hit me."

Kurt was also caught off guard by his wife's decision to leave: "Funny you should ask. She's remarrying this Friday. From the things she told me when she left, I was surprised. She said she did not think she could date, let alone this, you know. [Kurt had been divorced for two years.] I think there was something going on before. So it seems. She wanted out. She wanted me to move out first, and I told her no way—that I was staying. Since she left, she has kind of gone back to her childhood. She was married at sixteen. Even her own brother said he thinks she missed her childhood."

Paul's marriage ended following many attempts to reconcile: "We had trouble getting along from the start. We fought a little at first, and when the kids came, we continued to fight, though we kept a lot of stuff in. We tried counseling, and that helped for a while. Finally, I left. We got back together a few months later and then she left. We couldn't work it out. We were talking about it the other day . . . how our bad points trigger each other off. We're on O.K. terms but we just can't live together. We still love each other. When we split up things were bad, and now they are O.K. I picked the right girl to divorce."

A number of fathers were aware of problems but were sufficiently comfortable in the marriage to want to maintain the status quo. It is often easier to suffer with the known than to risk the unknown. There were also a number of fathers who were taken by surprise when their wives left. Either they had been burying their heads in the sand, or their wives were very good at disguising their unhappiness or their extramarital affairs. Some fathers recognized problems in the relationships and sought an end to the marriages themselves. Others, who arrived at that conclusion with their wives, described the breakup as a mutual decision. The reasons fathers give for their divorces relate to some of their later parental experiences and to their relationships with ex-wives.

## Reasons the Father Has Custody

Perhaps the most complex aspect of the father's experiences involves the issues surrounding the way he received custody. The issue of custody has changed greatly in the last few years as more states have initiated joint- or shared-custody laws, some of which make joint custody the arrangement of choice. In these situations, the judge must state why joint or shared custody was *not* given to both parents. This is a far cry from the days when the father typically became the noncustodial parent and did not feel he had a chance for custody if he wanted it. Recent research has shown that at least having contact with both parents can be the preferred situation for everyone.[3] The fathers in this study, however, were not involved in joint or shared custody. They had their children most of the time. (As noted, it is beyond the purview of this book to cover these issues in depth. A number of excellent sources are available to the reader interested in knowing more from a legal perspective.)[4]

One reason custody decisions are so complex is that there are three different parties involved: the mother, the father, and the children, as well as the judge, the lawyers, and other professionals. Depending on the situation, these first three parties have varying degrees of impact on the decision-making process. To understand what is involved in many custody decisions, it is necessary to look at each of these parties.

### The Mother

The research on single fathers corroborates the view of the fathers in this study that fathers receive custody most frequently and most easily when the mother consents. Gersick, for example, found that in 90 percent of the cases he studied in which the father gained custody, the wife had given pretrial consent (1979). If the father wants custody but does not have pretrial consent from the mother, the ensuing court disputes can be long, costly, and emotionally stressful for an already divided family. The fear of battle often scares off the father—and sometimes the mother—from seeking custody in the first place.

What deters the mother from seeking or fighting for custody is often the financial burden of paying for lawyers or the fear of losing the husband's financial support. In a preliminary analysis of data I am gathering on mothers without custody, I learned that many mothers give up custody because they do not believe they can afford to raise the children alone. On the other hand, the mother who behaves in an exemplary way, both morally and in her parenting, and who can afford to match the father's resources, is a formidable opponent in a disputed case, especially if she has not moved out of the house.[5] Especially with the fathers in this study, then, the mothers called the shots. In most cases the parents did not fight for custody through the courts.

## The Father

Even though the mother may hold the edge in some situations, the father has a number of pluses on his side in the event of a dispute. He usually has greater financial resources, which help him to hire a lawyer and to show he can provide a "better" home if he wins custody. He can make things hard for the mother by illegally threatening to withhold child support and alimony. There are also fathers who get custody without going to court by offering the wife a choice between her freedom and the children. If the man refuses to leave the house, and if she wants to get out badly enough, she may leave without the children. It is not surprising that many men who do not want the marriage to end in the first place are reluctant to give up the house, which then becomes a trump card in a bid to get the wife to come back or to hold on to something of value from the marriage.

## The Children

The rule of thumb here is that the older the children, the more likely it is that their wishes will be honored in case of a dispute. The sex and age of the children can be a factor, too, depending on the situation. Children often prefer to stay in their home. Thus whichever parent has remained in the home following the breakup may have the inside track with children who want to maintain their own continuity with their neighborhood, friends, and school.

These three parties have standing in the court; when there is a difference of opinion about who should receive custody, they may each have some form of representation, such as a lawyer or the special interest of the judge. When the father gets custody, it is often as an outgrowth of the desires of all three parties, with the father often believing he has the least control.

The fathers in this study gave a number of different reasons for why they have custody. Assigning these reasons to a few neat categories is an impossible task. A range of variables is involved, including the characteristics of the children and the parents. Therefore, after the responses given by the fathers on the questionnaire have been presented, some of the events that converge in parental custody decisions will be discussed.

## Fathers' Responses

The questionnaire asked the fathers how it was decided that they would have custody. Fourteen different reasons were offered, including "other," for which they could write in a response. The fathers could check up to two answers that they thought were most applicable. Some of the answers overlap.

The top six answers given were as follows: (1) by mutual agreement, (2) because the children picked him, (3) because he offered a more financially and emotionally secure home, (4) because the wife was unable to handle the children, (5) because he won a custody suit, and (6) because his wife deserted the family.[6] These answers are not mutually exclusive. A father's response that custody was decided by mutual agreement could be linked with any of the other reasons except for the father winning a custody suit. Further, getting custody by mutual agreement can mean a number of things to both the father and the mother. Although it definitely means the mother did not fight the settlement in court, it does not indicate the extent to which she opposed the custody decision, nor does it indicate the extent to which the father wanted custody. This is a vitally important point. Remember that during their marriages, many fathers became more involved parents as a reaction to the mothers' abdication of this role. The way the father gets custody often follows a similar course. The responses are as follows (fathers could have given more than one response):

*How Was It Decided You Would Have Custody?* (N = 1,136)

| | |
|---|---|
| By mutual agreement | 416 |
| The children picked me | 299 |
| I offered a more secure home | 247 |
| My wife could not handle children | 223 |
| I won a custody suit | 221 |
| My wife deserted us | 219 |
| We agreed I was the better parent | 158 |
| My wife did not want a court fight | 122 |
| My wife wanted a career | 93 |
| My wife was too ill to take care of the children | 56 |
| My wife remarried | 34 |
| The children needed a male role model | 30 |
| I abducted the children | 19 |
| Other ("she was unstable," "she did not love us," "her new husband said no") | 74 |

*Maternal Consent on a Continuum*

It is not solely the father's active pursuit of custody that enables him to get it. It helps a great deal if the mother relinquishes custody. The circumstances under which she may relinquish it vary. In the previous chapter, Peter, and the children who speak for Gail, disagree on why Peter got custody. But they agree that it was by maternal consent. It may be helpful to imagine the amount of maternal consent involved in the mother's giving up custody along a continuum. This conceptualization is being presented to point out the various degrees to which a mother may "willingly" be giving up custody. At one end of the continuum could be placed the 221 mothers who lost custody in court. Clearly they did not give up custody willingly or by mutual agreement. At the same time, the matching fathers fought for it. On the other end are those mothers who did not want custody at all. These are mothers who decided, for personal reasons or for the welfare of the children, that they did not want to be raising the children on a full-time basis. Mothers who could be placed in this category were those who deserted the family, those who wanted a career unimpeded by domestic responsibility, and those who agreed the father was a better parent.

The remainder of the custody decisions fall somewhere in the middle and might be described as being allocated by "reluctant consent." These include cases of mothers who do not have the children because their children picked the father, because the father offered a more secure home, because the mother wanted to avoid a court battle, or because she could no longer handle the children. Although in some cases these mothers did not lose custody of the children in court, they also did not voluntarily, willingly, or happily give them to the father. They were faced with a situation with no desirable alternative. Perhaps they could not financially afford to prolong the battle, or they thought it would be detrimental to the children. Some may have wanted the children to get to know their father. These mothers are different both from the women who willingly gave up custody and from those who lost it in court. This discussion shows some of the issues involved in trying to discern whether a mother has given up custody by mutual agreement. The role of the mother's feelings is important because, in many cases, her feelings affect the father's success in seeking custody.

To further understand the reasons for a father getting custody, these answers need to be considered within a framework of the father's situation, his parenting abilities, his desire for custody, his financial stability, and the pressure he is able to bring to bear. Most of the fathers, responding to a separate question, said they wanted custody very much. Only about one-quarter said they wanted joint custody or did not want custody at all when the marriage ended. The reasons they wanted custody of their children reflect a wide range of situations. The reasons are similar to some of those given in the previous discussion concerning why they got more involved in parenting. Some men wanted their children in order to preserve a sense of family they thought they were losing with the breakup of their marriages. Others wanted custody because they believed in themselves as competent parents and because they loved their children. Still others wanted their children in order to get back at their ex-wives or to save money. Finally, some men received custody against their will. Each of these groups will be discussed separately.

### Preserving a Sense of Family

Fathers in this group may not have had their children when the marriage first ended and may have sought custody when they realized they felt incomplete without the children. Other fathers in this group knew they wanted to preserve a sense of family when the marriage was starting to unravel. These fathers may have taken specific steps to improve their chances of keeping the children. For instance, they may have become more involved in household chores, child rearing, and community activities. They may have gained custody for a variety of reasons that are matched by the mothers' reasons for losing it.

### Belief in Their Parenting Abilities

These fathers were more likely to have been deeply involved in parenting from the beginning. They also may have become involved in parenting as they saw their wife slowly abdicating that role. The love they feel for their children is often their chief motivation to seek custody. They also may have gained custody for a variety of reasons, but they are more apt to have gained it because of maternal consent. A wife who sees the father as competent and involved may find it easier to relinquish custody voluntarily.

### Desire for Revenge or to Save Money

Most men do not admit to this reason when interviewed, so it is difficult to know how many fall into this category. Revenge may be a motivating factor for many of the fathers seeking custody in the first place, but a good judge can often discern this and block such fathers from gaining custody. In addition, after fathers have sought custody for a while, they may realize they really have to want it in order to receive it and maintain it. Once their anger has cooled, many decide revenge is not a sufficient motive for seeking custody.

Only two fathers who were interviewed talked about the financial benefits of having the children live with them. Jan, whose situation was described earlier, cannot afford to return custody of two of his three children to his wife. If she wins the current court battle, he will have to pay her $100 a week. He now receives $12 a week from her. If he loses, he would not have the expense of caring for his two children, but he also would lose $112 a week, which would disrupt the life-style he shares with his third child. Almost all of the other fathers interviewed said it was ultimately more expensive to have their children than to pay child support.

*Against Their Will*

In this situation, the father may have come home one day to find that his wife had deserted the family. Not wishing to be sole custodian, but left with no choice, he reluctantly agrees. He is neither psychologically nor emotionally prepared for the role. Fathers whose wives became ill, physically or mentally, may also fall into this category. Reluctant warriors, they struggle with their new role.

These fathers can be contrasted most sharply with the father who has won custody in court. This father has battled for his children. He wants them and has proved to a judge that he is qualified to raise them. He is prepared for the role.

Mendes (1976a) has dubbed these two different groups the *assenters* and the *seekers*. She found that the assenters—those fathers who had custody thrust on them—do not adapt as well to the demands of parenthood as do fathers who actively sought the role. Yet the issue of custody—both relinquishing and acquiring it—is sufficiently complex to make this categorization apply in only some cases. Although the findings discussed later in this book generally support Mendes's contention concerning the seekers and the assenters, this approach to categorizing fathers who seek custody may be slightly oversimplified.

## Other Findings

From the various answers given for why fathers have custody, a few other points can be made. It is shown that 20 percent of the fathers won custody following a court battle—a figure nearly twice as high as that cited by two other studies of single fathers. Those studies, completed in the 1970s, do not reflect the change in attitude since then—in men's belief that they can win custody if they actively seek it, and in women's desire to fight for it. Two trends may be converging here that result in more court battles. Until recently, men did not seek custody because they thought they had no chance to win it. Now they are more apt to seek it. At the same time, women who do not want to give up custody voluntarily may be inspired to fight for it because they can more easily afford a court fight than before as a result of increased job opportunities. It also may be that women, perhaps because of the women's movement, are less willing to give up what they want. These changes for both men and women may lead to more disputed cases in the future.

Two percent of the fathers abducted their children. This figure may be low, since some men may wish to protect their custody situation and not report an abduction. The results of gaining custody this way can be tragic. Whenever a parent snatches a child, enormous emotional upheaval follows. The child may not understand what is happening and may miss the original custodial parent, his home, and his friends; the child may lose temporary or permanent contact with all of them. He or she may become confused or anxious by the new surroundings and by a new level of anxiety in the abducting parent. Often the original custodial parent does not know who took the child, and may call in the police and the FBI. That parent has to deal with the loss of a loved one and the uncertainty about the child's whereabouts. The parent who did the snatching may have to embark on the life of a fugitive, moving from state to state, taking a new job and a new name.

One story illustrates this. A father who completed the questionnaire for the study accompanied the return envelope with a $10 bill and the following message: "Place an ad in the A.M. newspaper in [a midwestern town] saying, Attention, [fictitious name]. Call [this author] at the following number." The father, who had abducted his child, wanted to talk to me about his situation but did not want to reveal any information about his whereabouts except for the name of his home town. After the ad was placed, the man called to give his side of the story. He said that parents who abduct their children have been portrayed in a negative light, and he wanted to set the story straight. He said that ten years ago, when his daughter was four, he filed for custody and lost a court battle. The next day, when visiting his daughter, he asked her if she wanted to live with him. Surely not understanding the ramifications of the question, she said yes. He then packed their things and drove a thousand miles before stopping to make a new life for himself and his daughter in a new town. In the ten years since, the girl has never spoken to her mother. The father calls the mother occasionally to reassure her about the child's well-being, but not to reveal her whereabouts. Now a teenager, the daughter increasingly has been asking the father to let her speak with her mother. The father was proud of his accomplishments in his new life and felt little remorse over what had happened. He felt justified because he believed he had lost the court case unfairly. Despite the father's presentation, the human suffering in this situation is obvious.

The answers on the questionnaire also shed light on the issue of women who give up their families to pursue a career. According to the findings, the wife's career choices affected fewer than 10 percent of the cases. This small percentage shows that mothers who do not have custody do not seem to be strongly motivated by the need to pursue a career instead of raising a family.

Understanding the fathers' custody situation involves knowing how the father achieved custody, knowing broadly what motivates him to want it, and understanding whether he wanted it. It also involves knowing why the wife relinquished custody or lost it in court, and what her experiences are. The individual stories that follow provide examples of how some fathers have actually gained custody and what they went through. On the negative side, the stories include tales of abduction, split families, and children shuffling back and forth. There are also decisions concerning custody that seem to involve caring and forethought and that were handled optimally for everyone.

Ken, raising an eleven-year-old daughter, related this story: "My daughter chose to stay with me. Her mother did not ask her to move in. She was up there living with her mother. She was only eight years old. My daughter was expecting me to go south to visit her for the winter. When I first arrived for the visit she wanted to stay with me. I said O.K. I did not know if her mother would allow it. I asked her mother, and she said yes. I did not want my daughter's hopes to be built up, or mine, and I did not know until the last minute that it would be all right. Actually, I was down for the holidays and was going to leave five days later, but I was so afraid that her mother or someone in her family would talk her out of it, or not let her come, that I just rushed in and said we had to leave. I did not kidnap her, but I got her out fast. My ex-wife has remarried and sees my daughter every summer."

Slim, a policeman from Kentucky, said: "My son originally decided to stay with me, and my daughter went with her. Now both are with me. I felt I could supply a good home and they could stay in their home and go to school. If they had moved in with her, they would have had to have started over again with friends and everything."

Marcus gained physical custody of his two children when his wife moved out. His mother moved in for a short time and helped. Meanwhile, his wife got a job and an apartment. She wanted the children. Joint custody was arranged. All was working well until she remarried and moved 2,000 miles away. To everyone's regret she had to give up sharing the children. The separation from her has been hard for the children but they prefer staying in their home town to moving. She writes and calls frequently and they visit her on holidays.

Leonard was in nearly the opposite situation: He admitted to having abducted his child three years ago. When a lawyer told Leonard he had no chance of winning custody, Leonard took his seven-year-old son, Paul, and moved to a different city in the same state. Leonard took Paul because he believed Paul was better off with him than he would have been with his wife. He explained to his son that he and his mother could not stay married, and that Paul would be better off living with him. Leonard said his wife hired a private investigator to track him down at first, and then fought him in court for many months. Finally she gave up fighting. The son and his mother see each other infrequently and have occasional contact on the phone. Leonard's desire to have custody, his belief that Paul would be better off with him, and the lawyer's pessimistic outlook on his chances all helped motivate the abduction.

Leonard admits to feeling a little guilty but quickly adds that his son is better off with him. Incidentally, Leonard had to quit his job in the courthouse because he was afraid the judge who had tried his case would recognize him.

Sheldon, an engineer with three sons, has his children "because of an [paternal] instinct. I did not want the marriage to end and refused to leave the home. That forced the confrontation. She had to choose. She wanted out and so I got the children and the house. At first I got two of the children and one wanted to go with her. Then he came back with me and one of the ones I had went with her."

Having the children go back and forth between parents or having them split up, as disruptive as it may be, is not uncommon. The father described earlier who reported having a very good relationship with his wife now—the one who said he had picked the right girl to divorce—had such a situation, in which the children were first taken care of by their mother and then, following a reconciliation, by their father. The father wanted the children because he felt close to them. The mother, who was embarking on a new career, recognized the bond the father and the children had established while she was working nights and thought it would be better for the children to stay with him. She also felt the atmosphere in the small town where they lived was more conducive to raising children than that of the large city where she worked and to which she was about to move.

Gary, a mail carrier, describes his desire to live with his family: "In 1975 I did not have the chance to get custody as a man. My son wanted to stay with me, and she [his wife] allowed it. My daughter wanted her mother. My family was a very important part of my life, and that is why I pursued it. I did not want to give up the rest of those things that were important to me. I thought I was a good parent and did not feel her behavior was conducive to raising kids. I felt I was a better parent. At the time, the only way to get kids was to have them testify. If you really care about them, you don't want to do that. At the time, you just could not win otherwise. The lawyers say to men, 'You cannot get it,' so many men don't go after it. Many men do not want to assassinate their wives' characters, and many men do not want to involve the children in that either. I threatened, cajoled, and fought, and did everything I could to get them without going into court. It finally worked.

"Fathers are damn lucky if they have custody. It depends on the circumstances. You have to be lucky or the woman has to not care at all. I put pressure on her by threatening to fight, that there would be a war. More fathers would seek custody if they thought they could win it without hurting the child."

One father, Stephen, went through a long series of investigators and detectives before he could find sufficient grounds to get custody of his children through the courts. Nevertheless, he lost the court battle. The next day he heard from his wife that she was going to take the children and move out of state with another man. Stephen got a restraining order to keep her and the children in the state. She stayed for a year and a half, and then he got documentation that she had exhibited immoral behavior. He went back to court and won. Stephen wanted his children, but his desire for them was intensified because he believed she was not taking good care of them.

The quality of care the children receive from the mother is frequently mentioned as a reason for getting custody. Another father provided a similar story. He said: "The standards of my ex caused me to want to raise my daughter. [His ex-wife had run off a few times during the marriage.] She was not caring for her, so I wanted to do it. I never thought of raising her before the divorce, but when it happened, I wanted her. When I accepted the marriage was going to end, which I, at first, did not want to accept, I decided I wanted her. My ex had a daughter from her first marriage whom I adopted. When we got divorced, she went with her. Now she has remarried, and I do not know where she is." This was echoed by a father who said simply: "Five years ago I won the case. The children were not being properly cared for. I couldn't take it any more, so I got them."

Sometimes, following a divorce, fathers establish their own life without the children and then take the children in when they come knocking. Fred gained custody of his fifteen-year-old son two years after the son had left with Fred's ex-wife: "He showed up with his suitcase and jeans in arm and said, 'Dad, I want to live with you.' I did not have any experience, but it was okay with her. We never went to court."

Don was on his own for a year before his children came back: "I am raising them because she moved to another city, and they did not like it, and they did not like the stepfather. They came back because they wanted to stay where they were raised. And I am a little easier on them than she is."

There are also situations in which the wife wants to go off and find herself, and the husband becomes a willing partner in the arrangement. The children may be choosing the house, not the parent. John tells this story: "She wanted out. She wanted me to move first, and I told her no way . . . that I was staying. When she left, I don't know if she really wanted them at that time or thought it would be a hardship for her. We sat down to talk and she had nothing . . . no job or anything. I think it was planned for me to have them before she left. We sat down and talked with the children when I refused to leave because there was no reason for me to leave. I had been very active with the children and the community, and she even told me I was a very good father and husband. She knew they would be safe with me since I was from a broken home and knew how to cook, wash, and iron. I taught her most of it. She was going to leave and had no place to go except where she was going to work in a motel. So she did not have any facilities for the children. We both had our say with the children, and they wanted to stay in the house, and whoever was going to stay in the house that's who they were going to stay with. It was kind of a mutual arrangement."

One final story from a father who worked as a salesman. He was left with a son and daughter by his wife who thought she had missed something in life. What she wanted did not include her family: "My wife felt she had other, more meaningful things in life to do rather than be a mother or wife. She wanted to go out and have fun in life. She found someone to do that with after she left."

These stories paint a variety of pictures of how men end up with their children. In many cases, it is the wife's desire not to have custody that plays a major part in the father getting the children.

## Fathers Who Were Deserted by Their Wives

The group of fathers who gained custody because their wives deserted them (20 percent of the sample) was selected to see whether there were any differences between their situations and those of the other fathers in the study. Some interesting patterns emerged that show that these father's situations during the marriage, as well as after they obtained custody, set them apart from the others.[7]

Fathers who were deserted by their wives are likely, during the marriage, to have been more involved in such housework as cooking, cleaning, laundry, and shopping, as well as in disciplining the children, than were other fathers. It may have been this involvement that played a part in the wife's leaving. The wives may have felt more comfortable with their decision to desert because of the father's involvement. At the same time, the father may have gotten more involved in these areas, as discussed previously, because of the mother's abdication of these responsibilities during the marriage.

These fathers also had wives who were more involved in the role of breadwinner than the other fathers in the study. For example, a quarter of the wives who deserted were sharing in the role of the breadwinner during the marriage—a much higher proportion than was found among the rest of the sample. The wives who deserted were more likely to have a viable career option that made it easier to leave the marriage without being financially dependent on the father.

The reasons for the divorce given by the fathers whose wives deserted also differed significantly from other groups' responses. These fathers were much more likely to say the divorce was due to infidelity and less likely to give shared reasons. This was not surprising, since the conditions surrounding a desertion by a spouse are more apt to involve the act of infidelity, which is associated with behavior that was usually not mutually agreed on. The connotation behind desertion is just that—that the father did not expect it and had not planned for it.

Also, these fathers most likely had a lower income. Money can often be a significant factor in the breakup of a marriage. The mothers, by deserting, took a route out of the marriage that may have reduced their chances of getting financial support, rather than trying to work out an amicable settlement. Because they had less money, these women may have believed they had less to lose by leaving. At the same time, it must be remembered that these wives are more likely to have an income of their own. This would make them less dependent on their husbands for income and more likely to view leaving as an option.

Once the father had achieved custody, a number of other differences appeared in the experiences of this group of fathers. Fathers who were deserted were less likely to be satisfied with their social life. Nearly half of these fathers had wives who were unfaithful, a situation that may make socializing more traumatic now for the father than if the marriage had ended for some other reason. These fathers also felt less satisfied with their relationship with their children and with themselves as parents. In a desertion, there has probably been less time to prepare for taking over household responsibilities and child care.

It is not just the father who is being deserted. The children also feel abandoned and may resent both the mother and the father. It may be harder for the father to establish a relationship with them because of the emotional turmoil following their mother's desertion. The suddenness of the desertion throws everyone off and makes adapting to a new family setup much more difficult.

As might be expected, these mothers remained significantly less involved with the children following the desertion than did other mothers. With the desertion, many women left the state or went off with another man, who may have discouraged contact. Anger on the part of the father and children also may have discouraged the mother from contact. Over one-third of these mothers were described as not being involved at all with the children, compared with one-sixth of the other mothers.

The desertion of the wife also affects the father in the workplace. Nearly twice the percentage of fathers who were deserted found working very difficult, compared with the other fathers. Having good child care while the father is working is an important part of the father's satisfaction with his work life. Not having the wife involved after the divorce means less help with child care, less possible income support, and less helpful advice on how to raise the children. These fathers, because they are earning less money, have fewer options for child care. All these factors add up to create a more difficult situation for the father who works.

Thus the father who is deserted by his wife is apt to have been more involved in the housework and child care during the marriage, to be earning less money, to have a marriage that ended because of infidelity, to have a wife who is less involved with the children after the breakup, and to have less satisfaction in a number of parenting areas. These are the fathers who have gone through the most difficulties and are in the most pain. Their children also feel uncertain about their situation. They are apt to suffer from feelings of rejection and loss, which, coupled with the father's feelings, exacerbate the demands placed on the coping abilities of the family.

## Three Profiles

In summary, three profiles of the fathers' paths to custody will be presented. These profiles include the reasons the marriage ended, whether the father sought custody, and the reason he got it. These profiles are meant to encapsulate much of what has preceded.

### Profile #1

The father divorced his wife for shared reasons. He accepts some of the responsibility for why the marriage did not work out. He may feel that he and his wife were incompatible, that they could not communicate, or that they grew apart. He does not feel too angry at his wife and sometimes feels very positive about her as both a mother and a wife. He wants to raise his children because he loves them and because he does not want to lose what was left of his family. He did not pursue custody vigorously because he did not see a great need for the children to be raised by him instead of his wife. If he had viewed his wife more negatively, he might have pursued custody more actively. He received custody largely through mutual agreement. He and his wife agreed that he offered a more secure home and that he would be the better parent. The mother relinquished custody without much guilt and believes the father is a good parent.

### Profile #2

The father's marriage broke up because of his wife's infidelity. He wants to raise the children for a number of reasons. To some extent, he wants to maintain a sense of family. He also wants his children for revenge—as a way of paying his wife back for the hurt he endured because of her infidelity. He thinks his wife is immoral and/or incompetent. This father threatened to fight vigorously for custody. The wife made some attempts in court and then backed off. In this situation, the father moved into many of the parenting responsibilities during the marriage as the wife abdicated her responsibilities to pursue other interests. Angry feelings and distrust for the wife are the emotions most often felt by the father.

### Profile #3

The father's marriage ended because of the wife's problems and because she left. The father does not feel he is to blame for the breakup. The blame, if he sees any, is the wife's. Sometimes the father sees her behavior as occurring outside his realm of control; that is, she had needs that had to be met but that had little to do with him. The father in this situation wanted the children because he believed they needed him. He felt the need to fill a void left by the mother, whose problems made it hard for her to handle the children. He also pursued custody because he thought he had a good chance of getting it. The mother left the marriage and the children and then decided she wanted the children. The father balked at that and took steps to ensure that he retained custody. He got a court ruling to guarantee that he would keep the children. The judge believed the father was the better parent and decided the children should not be moved from home to home. The children wanted to live with the father. The father feels indifference towards his wife once he feels in control of the children.

These profiles are meant to give a general perspective on the way fathers end up with custody and some of their experiences along the way. In some cases, there is overlap. The father's experience is still heavily dependent on what the wife does, according to what these fathers have reported. He often takes his cues from her. According to the available data, these fathers did not enter their marriage as an unconventional type of man. Rather, events occurred, often instigated by their wives, that resulted in their ending up with custody. A number of factors converged that had to do with the man's openness to being a single parent, the mother's desire to relinquish custody, or her perceived incompetence, the children's wishes, and the idiosyncrasies of the court system if custody is disputed. What happens when the father begins raising his children alone will be described next.

## Conclusions

The intent in this chapter has been to describe the processes these fathers have gone through in getting custody. Because of the focus on the father's side of the story, some points need to be made to balance the impression the reader may be left with. First, as stated already, we are hearing one-half of the story. Second, because single mothers with custody are more prevalent, I have not dwelt on their situation. Yet we know, and it is shown in chapter 10, that mothers have situations that would also not provide a very pretty picture. That is the nature of divorce.

The information about the fathers in the study is valuable if we are to gain a better understanding of fathers and mothers. Both can be the victims and the victimizers.

# 4

# In the Home: Housekeeping and Child-Care Arrangements

When a father starts raising his children alone, the issue requiring the most immediate attention is the home. Regardless of the emotional adjustments the father and the children have to make, everyone has to be fed and clothed. Secondarily, child-care arrangements have to be made and the home has to be cleaned.

Two common assumptions exist about the father who has to run the household: that he will not do it well and that, if possible, he will use outside help, either his relatives or a housekeeper.

There is good reason for these assumptions. Traditionally, men have left the bulk of the housekeeping—especially tasks such as cooking, cleaning, and laundry—to the wives, while they have tended to share the responsibility for the shopping. The child-care arrangements have also been left to the wife. It is in these areas that family responsibilities seem to divide the most often along gender-related lines. Although men now are more involved in these tasks than ever before, there is a great deal of research confirming that the wife is still the primary caretaker of the home and children. Even when both parents work full time, the wife does most of the housework and takes responsibility for the child-care arrangements.[1] Despite the expressed desire of the so-called new man to share the housework and child care equally with his wife, in fact he does not do so. Blumstein and Schwartz (1983), in their book, *American Couples,* write: "Working wives do less housework than homemakers, but they still do the vast bulk of what needs to be done. Husbands of women who work help out more than husbands of homemakers, but their contribution is not impressive. Even if a husband is not employed, he does much less housework than a wife who puts in a 40-hour week" (pp. 144–145). Perhaps to avoid the drudgery of housework, or perhaps to maintain some dominance, men have successfully held on to the image of themselves as being incompetent in the kitchen, a threat with a washing machine, and lethal with a vacuum cleaner. Women, at the same time, are partners in this dance. They maintain their hold over the housekeeping and child care—perhaps as a way of trying to prove, if they are working, that they can do it all, and perhaps as a way of dealing with guilt about not being home all the time.

Housekeepers are also believed to be the father's salvation. A look at some television images of single fathers that the baby boomers grew up with shows where this assumption comes from. Fred MacMurray in "My Three Sons," John Forsythe in "Bachelor Father," and Brian Keith in "Family Affair," always had a family member or a housekeeper to run the show while they worked. But it is more than television programs that feed this assumption. Because men are the primary wage earners in most families, it is believed they will be able to afford the luxury of outside help.

These assumptions of incompetence and the need for housekeepers do not hold up when applied to the custodial father. The fathers in this study were more like Dustin Hoffman's portrayal of Ted Kramer in the film *Kramer vs. Kramer*. The first morning after his wife has left him, Kramer burns the French toast. During the movie, the apartment loses some of its initial tidiness and luster. By the end of the movie, however, Kramer is shown to be a competent cook who gets help from his son. This is similar to what many fathers reported in the study. After an initial period of mayhem, they established a routine and adapted comfortably to the demands of the housekeeping. They did not use outside help to a great extent; when they did, it was usually at the beginning of solo parenting. In addition, most of the fathers feel comfortable with the child-care arrangements they have made for their children when they are not home.

This chapter will look at the father in his home. Attention will be paid to how the housework is divided up, the effect that the age and sex of the children in the home has on how much work they do, and the role that outside help plays. The ease the father feels with housework will also be examined, as will the arrangements the father makes for child care.

## Who Did the Housework During the Marriage

As mentioned in the previous chapter, the fathers in this study left most of the housework to their wives during their marriage. Only about one father in nine reported that he was doing more of the cooking, cleaning, or laundry than his wife; only one in five said he was doing more of the shopping. Most often the wife was doing these chores; occasionally they were shared. It is important to consider these responses in order to understand single fathers. Even though these were fathers who ended up with the children, the degree of sharing of household responsibilities during the marriage did not deviate greatly from the norm. The relationships in these marriages, most of which began in the 1960s, followed the traditional path for the completion of family chores: The wives did the housekeeping while the husbands did the breadwinning.

## Who Does the Housework Now

Although fathers left much of the housework to their wives during their marriages, they had to decide how to handle the chores when they began raising their children alone. The fathers had four options. They could do the chores themselves, share them with the children, turn them over to the children or some other family member, or—if their income allowed it—hire outside help.

Fathers received the most outside help in the areas of cooking and laundry, but in no instance did the use of outside help apply to even as much as 6 percent of the sample. (The use of housekeepers may be infrequent because the average age of the children was over eleven years old, an age at which they were old enough to take care of themselves. Also, fathers may hire housekeepers only at first, when they are most uncomfortable in their new roles.) Fathers are most likely to do the shopping and the cooking by themselves and to share the cleaning and the laundry with the children. These latter two chores are left up to the children because they carry the least potential danger and need the least supervision. They also are the least important to the smooth running of the home. Table 4–1 shows how the housework is shared in the families surveyed.

As might be expected, when it came to the amount of money earned, definite differences appeared between the fathers in the amount of housework they and their children did. Fathers who earned more money were more likely to use outside help. Fathers who hired someone to do the cooking had an average income of almost $33,723, compared with an average income of $28,000 for fathers who did the cooking themselves. For the cleaning, the differences were even more marked. Fathers who used outside help to take care of that chore earned more than $36,000, compared with an average income of $27,000 for fathers who did the cleaning themselves and $28,500 for fathers who shared the cleaning with their children.

## The Age and Sex of the Children and Housework

In most families, whether headed by one parent or two, as the children get older they take on more of the responsibility for housekeeping. Daughters may be groomed for certain roles and sons for others. For example, the girls may have to help out with the cooking, while the boys do the yard maintenance and trash removal.

**Table 4–1**
**Who Usually Takes Care of These Chores Now?**

|  | Father | Children | Shared | Outside Help | N |
|---|---|---|---|---|---|
| Cooking | 65% | 1.5% | 27.6% | 5.7% | 1,136 |
| Cleaning | 35.8% | 4.7% | 54.7% | 4.6% | 1,134 |
| Laundry | 53.3% | 5.2% | 35.9% | 5.5% | 1,133 |
| Shopping | 71.4% | 0 | 25.2% | 2.8% | 1,135 |

Note: Missing data account for there being fewer than 1,136 responses to some of the questions.

The findings of this study show that as children get older, fathers tend to relinquish sole control over tasks and instead to share them with their children. An exception is shopping; in only a few cases do the children take over full responsibility for that task. Many fathers, however, end up doing more housework than they really have to, perhaps because of feelings of guilt. As one father said: "I feel the children have been through enough. I feel bad about asking them to do their chores around the house. I ask them to do it, but I feel bad about it." The father who believes he has burdened his children already with the dissolution of the family does not want to make further demands on them.

Another reason some fathers stay so involved in housekeeping is that they may think they have to prove to the world that they can take care of their children on their own. It is a sign of strength to do it alone and not ask for help. By being central in the home in this way they are maintaining control. Using relatives, friends, or hired help weakens the impression. This is part of a stiff-upper-lip mentality that many of the fathers interviewed demonstrated when it came to handling problems. The fathers also may feel it is important to let the world know they are not going to expect more from their children than may be perceived as normal. They may not want to give the impression of working them too hard or depending on them too much.

In some instances, a father may have won custody in court and may feel a need to show both the judge and his ex-wife that his children are being well taken care of. The father in this situation may believe that if he expects too much from his children he might not be upholding their best interests and might be brought back into court, which would threaten the custody arrangement.

Although some fathers absolve their children of doing much housework, it was found that fathers raising teenage daughters got more help than did those raising teenage sons. Daughters were, in fact, twice as likely to help out around the house than sons. Peter and Susan's situation is one example. No difference in the help received was found among younger children.

This finding, which is described from the children's perspective in chapter 11, is further proof of the traditional upbringing of many of these fathers. They turn to their daughters to take care of certain traditionally female tasks, just as they had left these tasks to their wives. In this way, some daughters become mother substitutes. They may receive support for this from various sectors. First, their family and friends may see it as a natural shift and place a spoken or unspoken pressure on both the father and the daughters to adopt this pattern. Second, the daughters themselves may voluntarily fall into this role. They may have been doing a lot of housekeeping during their parents' marriage and may continue or increase their work load when the mother leaves. This could be a natural progression that is comfortable for them and that also pleases the father. Finally, they may be aware of the need to get the housework done, unlike a son who was not previously involved in housekeeping. In any case, the result is greater participation by daughters in housework.

One father talks about what happened in his household: "When my wife and I decided to get a divorce, my daughters, who were then in their teens, stayed with me. I don't know how it happened, but they began doing the cooking and the laundry, I did the yard and the trash. We never discussed it. Sometimes they shop. I don't know, I guess I could cook if I had to but I like them doing it."

In summary, fathers do a good deal of the housework themselves when they have custody, and do not rely on outside help. As the children get older, and especially if there are daughters, fathers get more help.

## Comfort in Housekeeping

Do fathers find it difficult to manage household chores without a woman around? Can they find happiness with a broom and a frying pan? One of the more surprising findings of the study was that most reported they felt comfortable in these areas. Housekeeping did not pose problems. Shopping was perceived as the easiest chore by the fathers, cleaning as the hardest.

The fathers' generally high degree of comfort with housekeeping may be an indication of a number of different factors:

1. *The relative ease of the chores themselves:* Housekeeping, when one puts one's mind to it, is not difficult. Men have been scared away from it by tradition. When they have to do it, they do not find it that hard.

2. *The diminished expectations that fathers may have for the quality of how the chores are completed:* Many fathers cope with the demands of housekeeping by lowering their expectations about the way the house looks or the quality of the meals. Many women find a measure of their worth as a mother in how neat the house looks and how well-kept their children look. Fathers, however, have not grown up with that message; when they gain custody, they do not put as high a value on these things. With lower expectations, they are more likely to feel comfortable with how the house is run.

3. *The relative ease of these chores compared with some of the other demands of parenthood:* Housekeeping is simple compared with some of the other tasks the father faces that involve situations over which the fathers have less control.

4. *The role congruence of housekeeping:* Keeping the house clean, for example, is something that involves only the father and the clutter in the home. No one else's expectations have to be considered. There is no boss to please and no ex-wife wanting to visit the children. The cleaning exists, it is stable in its demands, it is controlled by how the father feels about it, and do-

ing it produces tangible results. For these reasons, compared both with other aspects of parenthood and with other situations that present more complex role demands, housekeeping proves to be an area in which the fathers feel a good deal of comfort.

## Who Finds Housekeeping Comfortable?

Among the fathers who were not too bothered by doing the housekeeping, it was possible to distinguish characteristics of the fathers who experienced the most comfort. For instance, the fathers who had had the primary responsibility for the chores during the marriage were the most likely to experience comfort in those chores now. These fathers found the transition to doing housekeeping alone easier than other fathers did, as they already possessed knowledge about the washing machine, the vacuum cleaner, and the cooking. They had also figured out how to do these things while holding down a job, which is no easy feat.

Fred, a salesman from Virginia, is one example. While married, he had been doing the bulk of the housework and working full-time. He thought his experience with the housekeeping contributed to his obtaining custody. Fred said about his wife's leaving: "She knew they would be safe with me since I was from a broken family and knew how to cook, wash, and iron. Better, in fact, than she did. I taught her most of it. She was ten years younger than I was."

Henry provides a slightly different example of a man with prior experience. A fifty-year-old security guard from a rural Kansas town, he had spent a number of years in the army before getting married in his late twenties. He believes his army experience prepared him for taking care of the home when he ended his marriage. When he began raising his two sons alone, he read a lot of books on cooking and cleaning. Now, when he wants to, he can get his house "spanking clean." His sons help him with the cleaning and the laundry; he does the cooking alone.

At the other end of the spectrum is Charles, who lives in Chicago where he works as an electrician. He had no prior experience, and he stumbled around the house for the first few weeks after his wife left. He concentrated mostly on getting his four daughters presentable for school, while letting the appearance of the house slide. Eventually, like most fathers, he became comfortable as a housekeeper. Now he laughs at the way female friends he once went to for help come to him for advice with recipes. His children are also now old enough to help him out more with the chores.

Not only does prior experience and having older children help when it comes to housekeeping, feeling comfortable financially is also related to comfort with housework. Money is able to buy fathers more options that can contribute to greater ease in handling these chores. If there are greater financial resources, laundry can be sent out and housekeepers hired. For example, wealthier fathers use more outside help, which definitely makes a single father's life easier. Peter had no major problems with housework as long as there was a housekeeper. Problems began when the family took care of the cleaning by themselves.

One final point needs to be made about the use of housekeepers. Divorced and separated fathers may tend to use them less than widowers do. I conducted a small study of eighteen fathers raising their children following the death of their wives.[2] These men employed housekeepers to a much greater degree than the divorced fathers—in part, perhaps, because they may have felt less need to prove to the world that they could do the parenting and housekeeping tasks on their own. The income of the fathers in both studies was the same.

The fathers who felt comfortable with housekeeping were the same ones who felt successful in other areas of parenting. They gave themselves high ratings as fathers, tended to feel pleased with their relationship with their children, and did not report feeling trapped at home. These characteristics appeared in many of the fathers who reported they were doing well raising their children.

Fathers who sought the role of sole custodian also tended to feel more comfortable with the housekeeping. These were the men who were more psychologically prepared for that role and found the transition easier to make than fathers who did not seek the role of sole custodian.

The one recurring theme heard from the fathers is that the first few months on their own were difficult as they and the children struggled with the new situation and the loss of the mother. After this period, however, housekeeping did not pose great difficulty for the fathers.

The story of Alonzo is one example of what can happen. Alonzo is a manager of a medium-sized business in Colorado. Five years ago, his wife left him and his two children—a fourteen-year-old son and a seven-year-old daughter—on the eve of the son's birthday. Alonzo and his wife had been discussing the possibility of getting a divorce for months, but she gave him no advance warning that she was leaving when she did. First, he had to straighten out who was going to carry certain responsibilities around the house: "Initially, everyone had a piece of the action. The first night I thought, what the heck am I going to do? O.K., guys, a little family meeting here. Most of the burden went to my son and me, as my daughter was too young to help out. He was great. He practically raised her. He missed things after school to be with her. The neighbors helped out a lot, too. My daughter is twelve years old now, and my son has gone into the army. She cleans and does some of the cooking but still has problems. I'll call her and tell her to start dinner and what to do. Like, 'O.K., boil up some water and take the ravioli out of the freezer and start it at five o'clock.' Other nights, if she is busy with her schoolwork, I'll bring in food. Otherwise there is always good old frozen food. We are surviving but not having what I would call good old family eating, roast beef and things. Laundry? I did that most of the time until recently. Now she does it."

Alonzo had problems at first but has worked out a system that adequately meets his family's needs, even though he regrets not having family-style meals. Like many men, he forges through the problems that come up. Most men do not seem to be overwhelmed by the housekeeping tasks facing them as single fathers. With few complaints, they do what they feel has to be done. This approach—part of their male upbringing—may actually help reduce the strains the fathers experience. Not acknowledging problems that arise may make the problems easier to get through.

## Child-Care Arrangements

Keeping a household running smoothly involves more than just housekeeping. Appropriate child-care arrangements have to be made. This undertaking seldom can be assumed lightly. Placing a child in someone else's care or in an after-school program is something working parents often do with reluctance. Many of the fathers gave a good deal of time and thought to the arrangements they made for their children. If they found good child care, it paid off for them. The satisfaction they felt with child-care arrangements proved to be a key variable in their satisfaction in many other parenting areas. In other words, if the father thought his children were well taken care of, other things fell into place for him. The fathers in this study were basically pleased with their child-care arrangements; almost three-quarters of the men reported satisfaction.

The arrangements the fathers made for child care varied on the basis of a number of factors, including:

1. The age of the children, with teen-agers being left alone the most.
2. The father's income and the choices that income gives him for hiring people.
3. The presence of support systems—families, friends, and neighbors.
4. The father's impressions of the individual needs of the children, as children with certain personalities may need more supervision than others.
5. The father's feelings about the type of home life his children should have. Fathers who are more upset by the dissolution of the intact family make a greater attempt to be home with the children.
6. The father's work schedule.

In the study, child care arrangements were examined in two time periods: during school hours and after school hours. Most of the fathers reported that during school hours their children were in school. Fathers raising children too young for school tended to use day care and sitters. Forty-nine fathers were home during school hours.

Arranging child care after school is more difficult for all working parents. School is usually over by midafternoon; yet many parents do not get home until early evening. This often leaves a two- to three-hour gap, during which time some other arrangement has to be made for the child. The following table shows the fathers' responses to the question of where their children are after school. Fathers could check more than one response.

*Where Children Are after School*

| | |
|---|---|
| Father is home = 295 | After-school programs = 66 |
| Relative/friend = 225 | With father at work = 25 |
| Day care = 71 | Sitter = 185 |
| Care for themselves = 681 | Other = 37 |

Over half the fathers in the survey reported that at least one of their children is alone after school. With the average age of the children in the study being between eleven and twelve, this is not surprising. Children at this age are usually capable of taking care of themselves.

After school, the youngest children—those in the one- to four-year-old group, tend to be either with their father, with a sitter, or with a relative or friend. One-fifth of the children in the five- to eleven-year-old age group are left on their own. The high percentage of latchkey children (children who let themselves into their own home and are alone after school) in this age group indicates the difficulties working parents confront in making child care arrangements. Even someone who earns an average income of $28,000 a year—well above the national average for single fathers and more than double the national average for single mothers—will have difficulty finding someone to watch the children. Other studies on latchkey children show similar findings. A 1974–1975 census report—the last time this information was available from the Census Bureau— on daytime care of children of single mothers shows that an equal number of children of approximately the same age cared for themselves in the home.[3] More recently, it has been estimated that 5 to 10 million children are left unsupervised after school, and that many of these children are under eleven.[4] This is more a commentary on day-care availability in the United States than on the child-care arrangements that single fathers make. It shows that fathers are not immune to the problems faced by single mothers or dual-career families.

## Difficulties Arranging Child Care

It is most difficult to arrange child care for children in the five- to eleven-year-old range. Fathers raising children over eleven and those raising children under five reported much less difficulty. This is most likely due to the lack of clarity on the father's part concerning how responsible these children can be for themselves. Should a child who is seven, eight, or nine be left on his or her own after school? Some fathers believe their children can take care of themselves at that age; others do not. At a younger age, the issue is clear-cut: The children must be taken care of. In the older age range, the issue is also clear-cut because the children are more capable of taking care of themselves. But concern about children between five and eleven makes arranging child care for them more difficult and requires greater care in making judgments.

Neither the father's income, the sex of the children being raised, the number of children he is raising, the number of years he has had custody, or whether he sought custody has a relationship to the difficulty the father experienced in making child-care arrangements. The father's concerns about child care rest more with the age of the children than with any other variables.

## Conclusions

Housekeeping and arranging child care, when compared with other areas of adjustment for the father, proved relatively easy adjustments. The father's lack of experience in handling these matters during the marriage does not seem to have a great impact on the comfort and satisfaction he feels in handling them (although fathers who have had experience during the marriage do better). The reason for the ease in handling housekeeping is, most likely, that doing housekeeping and related home maintenance chores is not that difficult. The tasks themselves are not hard, and there is no question about who is in charge. The father does not feel uncomfortable doing the chores because of conflicting expectations placed on him. He knows they have to be done and proceeds with the tasks to completion, although he may have diminished expectations for the quality of the results.

These findings are different from the assumptions that exist about the father being incapable of running the household without the mother present and needing outside help. Even though men in intact families leave the bulk of the housework to their wives, it can be assumed that, after a short period of time alone, they would feel comfortable taking care of these chores. What this implies about married men who do not do much at home is that they are in an unspoken conspiracy with their wives to have the wives do the housework. There is much in society to reinforce this arrangement. Unfortunately, a sloppy house reflects negatively on the wife more than it does on the husband.

It was particularly interesting to learn that fathers get more help from daughters than sons. Despite the nontraditional nature of this parental arrangement, some things have not changed.

# 5
# Balancing the Demands of Work and Child Rearing

Most of the fathers in this study, when they were married, went to work each day knowing their children's needs were being taken care of by their wives. If the child was sick, the wife usually was at home to shuttle him or her off to the doctor. If the wife worked, she was more likely than the father to take time off. If school conferences or other special events happened during the day, the mother would attend; the father would show up only if his schedule permitted. Having the mother available freed the father to work as needed to support the family. Having her there enabled him to work overtime, to attend after-work meetings, and to do work-related travel. The father, who was raised in a time when status was measured by his success in the work world, could put everything into his job.

When the father ended up with sole custody, all that changed. He could no longer work overtime if it interfered with his child-care schedule. He could no longer earn the extra money he might need. Perhaps most significantly, he had to change his priorities. Instead of fulfilling the childhood goal of working his way up the career ladder and measuring himself by his success in the work world, he had to become a full-time parent and choose which of the two roles he was going to be most successful at: parent or worker. Many fathers found they could not do both well; one role had to suffer.

The adjustment the fathers experienced working while child rearing turned out to be one of the most difficult. Only one in five said working while child rearing was not at all difficult; the rest said it was somewhat or very difficult. On first impression, this finding is surprising. Men have been raised in our society, as in nearly all societies, to fulfill the worker's role. Nearly 90 percent of the men in this study reported that they had the primary responsibility for the breadwinning chores during the marriage. On closer examination, however, it is clear that, regardless of his experience in the workplace, when the father has sole charge of his children and the responsibilities of a worker, conflicts arise that make both much more difficult. These conflicts are, to some extent, unique to men.

Before discussing the difficulties single fathers have with working while child rearing, the role that work plays in most people's lives must be noted. Even without the demands of parenting, work can be stressful. Studs Terkel (1974), in his book on working, describes the stresses inherent in the workplace: "This book, being about work, is, by its very nature, about violence—to the spirit as well as to the body. It is about ulcers as well as accidents, about shouting matches as well as fistfights, about nervous breakdowns as well as kicking the dog around. It is, above all, about daily humiliations. To survive the day is triumph enough for the walking wounded among the great many of us" (p. xi).

Most adults who have held a job can agree with some or all aspects of this opening statement to Terkel's book. Certainly Peter, with his business ups and downs, would agree. The workplace itself can be a place of great tension, uncertainty, and inflexibility. During an economic downturn these problems can be exacerbated. Workers are under pressure to get ahead, to earn more money, to attain greater job status. Work is an integral part of the way a person feels about her- or himself. It is so important that in times of high unemployment there are also increases in mental-health problems and child abuse.

Our ideas of the importance of work are deeply ingrained. For the men in this study, the majority of whom were born in the 1940s, being a man meant being a breadwinner and supporting a family. Men were supposed to grow up and go off to work, where, it was hoped, they would excel. Women were supposed to grow up to be mothers and housekeepers. As mentioned earlier, Parsons defined the roles men and women fulfilled as the *instrumental* and *expressive* functions. The more the father achieved at work, the better off the family would be, because their standard of living would be higher. The roles of mothers and fathers were complementary and mutually exclusive. Most men deferred to their wives when it came to parenting issues; most women deferred to their husbands when it came to financial matters. If a father was transferred or had to move to find new work, the entire family went with him. Rarely if ever was the reverse true—that a father would find a new job because of his children's special needs or his wife's desires for a homemaking experience in a different city.

In this climate, the father's job became the controlling variable in the family's life-style. It defined where and how the family would live. The pressure on the father at the workplace could be enormous.

Recent years have seen a great change in the number of working women, but men's jobs still frequently control the family environment, with the mother's income often supplementing the father's. As mentioned, among married couples in 1981 (the most recent year for which data are available), only 11 percent include women earning more than men.

When a father begins raising his children alone, the stresses of the workplace do not go away. Instead, the responsibilities of child rearing present another job to cope with. This new job is often in conflict with the work the father does outside the home. Hence it is not surprising that working while child rearing was difficult for nearly four of the five fathers.

The research on single fathers has pointed out the difficulties many fathers experience trying to work while child rearing. Job mobility, earning power, freedom to work late, job performance, and job advancement are all negatively affected. Some fathers had to quit or were fired. One gave up working completely and went on welfare so he could be home with his child.[1]

## The Responses

What happens to the father when he gets custody? According to the questionnaire returns, the 1,136 fathers in this study reported experiencing a total of 2,158 different job changes. The changes experienced the most often were having to arrive late or leave early (35 percent), having to miss work (34 percent), and having to reduce work-related travel (32 percent). Another 27 percent reported that they did not have to undergo any work-related changes.

A few men underwent more drastic changes. Sixty-six men reported having to quit their job because of their parenting responsibilities, and 43 men reported being fired (see table A-15 for complete response rate). Harry described his experience with having to change jobs because he was raising a young child. He had been working very satisfactorily as a clerk, but when he began raising his two small girls after he and his wife separated, he ran into problems. He found that he could not take his three-year-old to his job, nor could he afford to hire someone to care for her. He described himself as "old-fashioned" in not wanting his child to be raised in a day-care center. Eventually he found a job as resident manager of an apartment complex. That position enabled him to work out of his home and to take his youngest child along on any maintenance calls he had to make.

Whereas Harry chose to leave his position for one that enabled him to be home more, Pierre, a Canadian father, was fired from his job as a trucker because he could no longer work overtime. Pierre said: "They have this bullshit that single parents can't work overtime. Well, I couldn't and I was fired because I couldn't." Pierre is now employed by the province in which he lives and, because of union rules, is not required to put in overtime.

Bob angrily described a similar experience: "Due to my health problems and stress from the divorce and raising the kids, I lost my job of twenty-two years. I think companies should have programs for people going through divorce because they do not understand the problems. They have programs for alcoholics. Why not for us fathers?"

In the film *Kramer vs. Kramer,* Ted Kramer loses his job because of his responsibilities to his son. He begins to miss important meetings, to turn in his work late, to accept urgent phone calls from his son during conferences. The outcome? A lower-paying job.

Having less income because of solo parenting means a number of adjustments for the father and his family.

One father, a policeman, worked the day shift on the force for a number of years. He also worked part-time in the evenings to supplement the family income. When he left his wife, he had to give up his part-time job and the extras that work had brought him. He was philosophical about the changes: "If you don't have it to spend, then you don't spend it."

Mark, a salesman who worked on commission, was not so amused by his changed circumstances. When he was married and had someone at home to take care of the children, he could attend sales meetings, take clients out to dinner, and travel. He was the typical salesman—always on the go. Like many people in sales, he knew that the more time he put into his job, the higher his income would be. At one time he earned well over $35,000 a year. Mark never had to worry about his children during the day because his wife, who did not work, was always there. When he ended up with custody, the family's life-style changed dramatically. Mark's income dropped by a third because he could no longer attend sales meetings or be as free about taking clients out to dinner. He had to sell the house, split the proceeds with his ex-wife, and move to an apartment. "I guess when the children are older, I'll be able to earn more again. But I sure hated to lose my house."

In addition to the financial adjustments, fathers must make psychological adjustments when they can no longer pour themselves into their career. An accountant in Virginia was very articulate about having to shift the way he viewed himself: "When I got out of school, I worked very hard trying to become the best. But then, when I got my kids, I was no longer the guy who was going to earn $40,000 a year by the time I was thirty-five. I was raising a seven- and a nine-year-old, and I had to completely revise my self-image. It has been damned hard." Another father, an engineer, said simply: "I'm stuck where I am. I can't move elsewhere. I can't go up. I'm stuck."

Another aspect of child rearing causes discomfort to single fathers. Fathers reported being upset about the loss of their ex-wife as a child-care provider. Not having the children home with their mother has meant reevaluation of the importance they may have placed on the nuclear family being able to take care of its own. Other child-care providers, such as day-care centers, become options that fathers grudgingly accept; but they feel their children are suffering, and this concern pulls them more and more away from work.

For the father who was under stress at work during the marriage even when his wife was taking care of the children, a new set of stresses appears when he must function as a single parent. The father who formerly defined himself as a worker first and a father second must shift his values, accept less income, change his view of himself as a worker, and try to adapt to conflicting demands. No longer can he chase the golden ring of success. He has to come to grips with his own upbringing, which has always pushed him toward bigger career goals. While his co-workers and friends move ahead, he may stand still or even take a step backward. This radical shift in the way he views himself at work is something that some single mothers, who may never have experienced the same emphasis on achievement in the workplace, do not have to deal with. In this way, single fathers differ from single mothers. Although the stresses involved in scheduling child care are similar, the strain of the role is a greater problem for the male.

Single mothers, of course, have a host of problems to which they must adapt. The picture for the mother who is working will be shown, in chapter 9, to be more difficult as she struggles with inadequate income and less job flexibility.

A few fathers who were interviewed welcomed this change in their priorities. They were unhappy with the pressures placed on them by their work and their upbringing. Being a parent first and a worker second has enabled them to enjoy their lives more and to learn more about themselves. When they were concentrating on work all the time, they were too busy to appreciate their children.

## Difficulty Working

What makes working more difficult for some fathers than for others? As might have been anticipated, the more job-related changes a father underwent, the greater the difficulty he experienced. As shifts in work schedules, reduced overtime, and missing work added up, work became harder and harder. Not surprising, the fathers who reported being fired or having to quit usually had the greatest difficulties.

Although one would think that lower occupational status, less education, and lower income would all be related to less job flexibility and hence more difficulty, this turned out not to be the case. There was no link between these characteristics and the difficulty of working while child rearing.

It *was* found, however, that although the actual income earned has no effect on the father's difficulties, a change in his income does. In other words, a father whose income falls from $25,000 a year to $20,000 a year will find things more difficult than will a father earning $16,000 a year who experiences no drop in income after the breakup. The fathers make ends meet with whatever they have; but when what they have is reduced, it is harder for them than if they did not have the extra money in the first place. Tom's story illustrates this: "Before the divorce, my wife and I had all the basics. She was working twenty hours a week. We could make ends meet. Not any more. Her income does not go to paying for the food like it used to. It goes for her own place. There just isn't as much." The problem is further exacerbated for this man because he cannot put in overtime at work. To do so, he would have to leave his children alone at night.

Fathers who did not seek custody but had it forced upon them, tended to find working—and many other aspects of parenting—more difficult. When the father does not want sole custody but finds himself thrust into the role— either because his ex-wife does not want the children or because she is physically or emotionally unable to take care of them—he may feel a great deal of anger about the interruption in his work schedule that child rearing introduces. He may not be psychologically prepared to assume the role of full-time parent. He may find himself unwillingly upsetting his work day and his career goals to take on the responsibility of his children. He may also feel guilt because of his feelings of anger. This makes his reaction to parenting much different from that of the father who willingly accepts his children with some idea about what that might mean for his career goals.

Younger fathers were more likely to find working and child rearing difficult than were older ones. This could be expected for two reasons. The older the father, the more experience he will have had at work and the greater his freedom to come and go as he pleases. He also may have become more indispensable to his employer over time, so that his boss may be more accommodating. The second reason is that the older father is more likely to be raising older children, who need less supervision.

Just as certain characteristics of the father affect his difficulty working, so do some of the characteristics of the children.

## Characteristics of the Children

When the research project began, I believed the sex, number, and age of the children being raised would all have an impact on the father's parenting experience. I learned that although the sex of the children being raised did not seem to make a difference in the degree of difficulty the father had working, the number and the age of the children did. Although most of the men were raising either one or two children, those fathers who were raising three or more—almost one-fifth of the sample—found working more difficult. This would be expected: The more children there were to raise, the more childcare demands there are. There are more parent-teacher conferences to attend, more doctor's appointments to make, and more phone calls to field from battling siblings. With one child at home, there is the potential for only one crisis at a time. For the father raising three or more children, the potential for crises is greatly increased.

The age of the children can be a factor, too. As discussed in the previous chapter, the father raising children in the five- to eleven-year-old range turned out to have the most difficulty working. It can be presumed that the reason for this is that this age group poses particularly tough questions for the father concerning children's ability to take care of themselves.

Even when elaborate and satisfactory child-care arrangements are worked out that allow the father to work as he would like, things tend to happen that throw everything out of kilter. Frederick, a manager raising a five-, a three-, and a two-year-old, was able to manage everything with his two oldest in day care and his youngest at a sitter's home. With the hours offered by the day-care center, he thought he had all bases covered. But when the two oldest became sick with chicken pox one day and were not able to go to day care for two weeks, he had to stay home with them. Because he missed so much work, he was fired. He now has a new job and a more understanding boss. Instead of being on salary, however, he is working on straight commission. He says he is not earning the kind of money he used to; as a result, his self-esteem has suffered.

Some of the fathers discuss their concerns about the children even when the children are past the age of needing constant adult supervision. James has been raising four children aged twelve through twenty for about two years. James said that he worries about his children even though they are older and even though he works only four blocks from his house. His oldest son, who is sixteen, works; but the twelve- and fourteen-year-olds are too young to work and too old to be watched by the twenty-year-old, who is looking for work. Summers are especially troublesome because the children are home for long periods of time.

Satisfactory child-care arrangements can go a long way toward helping the single father to adjust to working. Some men are able to go to greater lengths than others to assure that their children are well taken care of in their absence.

One man, who has had custody for five years, provides such an example. Samuel lives in one city but works in another, 100 miles away, where he has assumed responsibility for his father's business.

His son is eleven years old and attends school in their home town. Samuel commutes daily between the two cities by train. Because he runs the family business, Samuel has more flexibility than those fathers who have to answer to a boss. Yet he also has greater responsibility for management, which makes his job a stressful one. He has been able to arrange a system of beepers between the two cities that permits him to be called at a moment's notice if there has been some change in his son's child-care arrangements or if his son needs him. With this arrangement, he feels comfortable that his son is always being well taken care of.

Fathers adapt their work lives to the child-care needs of their children in a variety of ways. One father, who could not find a sitter for his children after school, remained in the army longer than he had planned to so that he and the children could benefit from the safer environment on the military base where they lived. Another father started a business at home, where he made seasonal gifts. Working out of his house, he was able to be at home when needed for his small children. In these diverse ways, fathers adjust their work lives and their home lives to find the best match between the two.

## Involvement of the Ex-Wife

The involvement of the ex-wife also affects how the father feels about his work experience. Just as she was important to the father during the marriage, when she helped him pursue higher career goals by taking care of the children, so too can she be helpful after the breakup. The more contact she maintains with the children, the easier it is for the father. The nature of the relationship that develops between the custodial father and the ex-wife is described in depth in chapter 8, but a number of advantages of a good relationship can be touched on here. There is a greater likelihood of child-care assistance, of financial assistance, and of the children being less upset by the divorce and hence less dependent on the father.

One case illustrates this point. Herman's ex-wife, Sue, lives in the same city as he does and takes their son on the weekends. Sue has lived with her mother and father since the divorce. About once a year, Herman goes to a week-long convention that is important to his career. During that time, his ex-wife takes their son. She works during the day, so the child care is left to her parents. Without the help of Sue and her parents, Herman might have had to miss some of these conventions in the three years he has had custody. It is easier for him to travel knowing that backup support is there.

In a minority of cases, an ex-wife who is very involved with the children can make working *more* difficult for the father. Tom, who for a variety of reasons does not like his ex-wife, gets phone calls from her while he is at work. She may call to change visitation or to suggest a new way of approaching a problem with one of their children. If she were not so involved, Tom would have to try harder to schedule child care; but he also would not be bothered by his ex-wife's calls when he is at work.

## The Need for Flex-Time

The survey permitted the fathers to write in what changes at work would make life easier for them as single fathers. Although nearly a third of the fathers who answered the question indicated that no changes were needed, almost an equal number expressed a need for some form of flexible work schedule. Fathers gave answers such as "being able to work shift work depending upon my kid's schedule," "being able to leave work if my child is sick," and "being able to bring work home." These answers can be categorized under the heading of *flex-time*—the ability to put in the required number of work hours on a flexible schedule that more closely meets the needs of the individual worker.

One father wrote that the lack of flex-time was the hardest thing for him about single parenting: "I've raised my son from the bottle and diaper stage. My life would not be complete without him. But it is hard when he gets sick and I can't leave work."

The need for flex-time increases as the adequacy of child care declines. Fathers who have good child-care arrangements do not feel as great a need for flex-time. Of course, the need for flex-time at work is not unique to fathers. In any situation in which both parents work, or there is a working single mother, it can be needed. A fictional example of some of the problems of a working parent was seen a few years ago in the film *E.T.* In this case it is a single mother who is raising her three children after her husband has deserted the family. With some trepidation and many instructions, because she cannot afford to miss work, she leaves her son Eliot home alone after he has faked a fever by placing the thermometer against a hot light bulb. Luckily, Elliot has the extraterrestial to take care of him. The situation, though amusing, did raise the issue of the problems facing parents when there is no one home to take care of a sick child.

Asking for flex-time or leaving work can be psychologically harder for a man than for a woman unless the woman is working in a traditionally male occupation. If the child is sick, the father may feel embarrassed by asking for time off, especially if his boss does not understand single fathers. The embarrassment may stem from having to ask for a favor—something men who go through life with a stiff-upper-lip mentality have trouble doing. It may be a greater burden for the father than for the mother because many women are hired at lower-status and lower-paying positions; their bosses know that taking time off for child care is a possibility. Unfortunately, that expectation often results in a different set of problems for women—such as not being hired in the first place or being given less responsibility at work. Equally unfortunate, when men are hired, it is not expected that they may have to leave work because of child-care problems. This expectation makes some fathers uncomfortable when asking for time off.

There is a relationship between the difficulty the father is experiencing at work and his need for flex-time. The fathers who were having the most difficulty working expressed the greatest need for workplace flexibility. The importance for single fathers of having a flexible work environment cannot be overstated.

Other changes the fathers expressed a need for at the workplace covered a range of situations. Some men complained they did not earn enough money to support their families. A few others, harking back to Terkel's view of the stressful workplace, wanted less responsibility at work. Suggestions included: less travel, fewer nights out with customers, less overtime, and shorter hours. Other fathers wanted more overtime so they could make ends meet, or more stable employment. Some dreamed of being self-employed, which was Peter's status. When business was good, it worked to his advantage. A few fathers mentioned wanting greater access to a telephone at work so they could speak to their children more often; some wished they could work closer to home.

Finally, a number of men wished they could receive more understanding both from their co-workers and their boss. For these fathers, having a sympathetic person to approach when there are problems can make the demands of working much more manageable.

The experiences of the fathers are not universally dismal. One father, in stark contrast to the men who reported being fired or having to quit, found a lot of support in the steel mill where he is employed: "I have a very good foreman. He knows my problems. His boss knows my problem. I talk with my immediate supervisor if I have a problem. They are pretty lenient. They don't like me missing work, but thank God the kids have not been sick where I would have to have missed a lot of time. Knock on wood. When I was going through the divorce, I had to go to court and take time off. They were pretty nice about that."

## Conclusions

The problems faced by the working single father are more than merely the logistical problems shared by all working parents. He has to change the way he feels about himself as a *man*. It is not simply that it is difficult to make work schedules and child-care schedules mesh. Many fathers believe that since they have become single parents, they have been sliding by at the job; they think they are not giving the boss his or her money's worth. Others think their bosses have not been understanding of their situation, and that too much is expected of them. Still others long to be self-employed, to be able to work less, and to be able to earn more money—desires they did not feel so acutely when they were married.

What many of the fathers cannot escape—and what does not feel good— is that they are not earning as much money as they used to, and that they are not able to concentrate on advancement. They had always believed they would be able to get ahead, to achieve status in the world through success at work and earning a decent income. Instead, they are achieving a different kind of status—that of being seen as being a good father. Although that particular status goes a long way toward making many men feel wonderful, to others, it is not enough.

Some fathers want it both ways. They want to be able to work at the same pace they did when they were married *and* to be the father they think their children need. They want to be like the so-called supermoms—women who try to excel both at a career and at motherhood, and often burn out in the process. They want to continue the professional climb while handling the home front. These men, being newer to the role conflicts of working and child rearing than many women, have not learned some of the survival skills that can prevent burnout. Their consciousness is still a few years behind that of some women who have figured out how to adjust to the demands of both worlds.

Other fathers more easily accept the fact that they cannot have things both ways. They have put their career aspirations on hold until their children are independent.

For almost all men, the voice that has always told them to get ahead, to earn money, can never completely be silenced. For some, however, it can be quieted for a few years.

# 6
# The Father's Relationship
# with His Children

A father from New Jersey said: "My relationship with my son is better than it ever was. We are very close. We touch a lot and say 'I love you.'" A father from Boston reported: "Things were tough at first, and they still are tough for my son. He's having school problems. But they are better than before and they are good between us." A father from Nevada wrote: "One daughter is doing well, but the other one is having a very hard time."

Regardless of the successes and failures of the fathers in the different areas of parenting discussed in this book, the most important area is the one in which the fathers have the most invested: their relationship with their children. It is the satisfaction the fathers derive from being with their children, their impressions of how the children are doing, and the way the fathers feel about themselves as parents that are the markers, from the fathers' point of view, of how this parental situation is working out. By the fathers' own accounts, things are going well. Eighty-two percent felt satisfied with their relationship with the children; 70 percent felt satisfied with how their children were doing in most areas of their lives; and 82 percent rated themselves "excellent" or "good" as a parent. Descriptions of the fathers' relationships with their children, the possible reasons for the high degree of satisfaction felt by the fathers in this area, and the characteristics that contribute to satisfaction with the father-child relationships will be presented in this chapter.

Fathers have not always been as involved in the home as many have become in the last decade. Examples of poor fathering abound in popular literature. Huckleberry Finn's father, saddled with the dubious pleasure of raising his undomesticated son, spends his time either drunk, committing petty crimes, or beating up Huck. Hansel and Gretel's pathetic father abides by the stepmother's demands to abandon his children in the forest so that the two adults can live. These are not two men who were supportive and nurturing figures in their children's lives.

Numerous research articles and books written in the last three decades have shown fathers to be peripheral compared with mothers in their involvement with their children. One source cites a study from the 1970s that found fathers spent an average of 37 seconds a day with their infant child in verbal play. In a second study, fathers were observed to average between one and two hours a day in housework or child care.[1] The two studies depict the father differently, but they are consistent in showing that the bulk of the housework and child care fall to the mother. In other research, fathers have been found to be viewed by their children as less affectionate, less accepting, and less emotionally responsive than mothers.[2]

The question of the degree of involvement of the father in child care in the intact family is different from the question of what kind of relationship the father is *capable* of developing with his child. The first question deals with what *is*, the second with what *could be*. There are many indications— even from research done in the 1970s, when the role of the father in the family had not evolved to the point it has today—that fathers can be adequately nurturant parents. Clarke-Stewart (1977), after observing fathers with their young children, concluded, "There is no research evidence that biological mothers are more effective than adoptive mothers or that women are more effective than men in caring for infants and promoting their psychological development" (p. 21). These findings concerning the father's ability to parent are amply supported by other research.[3]

The research on single fathers with custody tends to draw three conclusions about the types of relationships that develop between fathers and their children:

1. That some men have difficulty handling the emotional needs of their children.
2. That having sole custody has improved the father's relationship with his children.
3. That raising daughters poses unique problems for fathers.[4]

When the single father gains custody, he moves into a new realm of raising his children, one for which he may have had little preparation. A number of factors make building a good father-child relationship difficult. The father may be unused to handling his children's emotional ups and downs. He may not know what normal developmental stages for children are. He may be feeling angry and lost as a result of the separation and his new responsibilities. In many cases, his wife may have handled everything herself. Left to his own devices, he has to carry the full weight of the children's emotional, social, and physical needs.

As the fathers struggle to adapt, the children have a number of difficult adjustments to make as well. They are coping with the divorce, the loss of daily contact with their mother, a possible change in residence and new friends, and a change in the financial stability of the home. These factors, which add to the children's vulnerability, can make it doubly difficult for the single father to establish a satisfying relationship with them.

## The Fathers in This Study

Some fathers in this study were emotionally prepared to begin single parenting. These were men who had thought about custody, had wanted it, and planned out each step. They most likely had been fairly involved with their children before the breakup. At the other extreme, there were fathers who did not want custody at all, or who wanted it but were not prepared for it. They may have become parents without any advance warning, having had little previous experience in being alone with their children.

One example of a father who was prepared for single parenting is Henry, the security guard mentioned in chapter 4. Henry was married for thirty years before he initiated divorce proceedings three years ago against his wife, who was an alcoholic. Henry was prepared for single parenting both by the desire he brought to the custody arrangement and by the experience he had had in taking care of a home before he was married.

The relationship that developed between Henry and his sons is not atypical. His two teenaged sons wanted to live with him, and his daughter wanted to stay with her mother. The decision was worked out amicably.

Because Henry works the night shift, he does not spend much time with his sons. They see each other at breakfast before they go to school, and at night before Henry goes to sleep. When they were younger, they used to take bus trips together. As children grow up, however, their needs change, as does their relationship with their father. One of Henry's sons was trying out for the football team at the time Henry was being interviewed. That meant that even when Henry was not working, it was difficult to schedule time with his sons.

When discipline or school problems come along, Henry handles them the same way he handles his job—by laying down the law. Henry does not talk much, but when he does, his message is clearly understood. He has told his sons if they can find someone who treats them better than he does, they are welcome to leave. They have not left yet.

Henry describes his relationship with his children as "close" and, from talking with Henry, it seems to be close in a traditional male way. When they are together, there is an understanding and caring between the three men that they do not talk about a great deal. As with many men, actions speak louder than words; the fact that Henry indicated he wanted the children, and that they chose to live with him, says it all.

Henry wanted the marriage to end and even initiated the proceedings. He had thought about the children and offered all of them the chance to come with him. His sons' choice of him as the parent they wanted to live with may have heightened the sense of belonging and improved the quality of their relationship. Henry has a fierce sense of belonging to his children and having them belong to him. The atmosphere in the house, had his daughter come to live with them, would not have been the same—would not be as "male," Henry says. Maybe, however, there would be more verbalization of feelings and more time together. Henry is not sure.

Charlie, also mentioned in chapter 4, is living in almost the opposite situation. He was not at all prepared for the breakup. He has been raising four daughters since his ex-wife left him for another man a year ago. He was given only a few days notice that she was leaving, although he had had suspicions for awhile. The relationship he has with his daughters, in which he gets along better with some than with others, is also not atypical. He describes himself as a father who was not particularly involved with his children during the marriage. All four girls, whose ages range from six to fourteen, are doing well in school. Each has a different relationship with him. The two youngest enjoy being in his company, and he gets along well with them. The oldest is a handful. She grumbles about wanting to live with her mother, a matter still to be settled in the courts. Charlie is reluctant to give her up, as he does not want to break up the children. The fourth daughter fluctuates between joining the two youngest in games with Charlie and sulking in her room with her older sister.

Charlie has tried to shield his children from the animosity he and their mother share for each other. He wonders whether he has been successful with his oldest. She had felt the closest to her mother during the marriage, and she misses her mother the most. There is the possibility that Charlie tried to give her too many of his ex-wife's responsibilities when the marriage first ended. Issues surrounding housework remain a problem for them.

Charlie spends a little time alone with each child every day, which has helped his relationship with them. He says that problems are discussed very openly in the house and that everyone gets lots of hugs and kisses. In this predominantly female household, one would think Charlie would rule as king. Although he sets the tone, however, it is a tone that is greatly influenced by his daughters. He worries that he is deferring too much to his oldest daughter in an attempt to smooth things over with her. He tried that approach with his ex-wife, and it did not work.

Henry and Charlie are struggling, with various degrees of success, to establish a good relationship with each of their children. The abruptness of the mother's departure can make this struggle harder, especially in Charlie's case, in which his oldest daughter may be taking out on him the rejection she feels from her mother.

A separate area of questioning in the study, relating to this issue of preparation, inquired about the father's involvement in discipline and in doing activities with the children during the marriage. Many of the fathers reported sharing these two areas of responsibility with their wives. The more the fathers were involved in these areas during the marriage, the more comfortable they felt in them now that they had sole responsibility. As with the comfort felt by the fathers in housekeeping, previous experience pays off.

## Why Fathers Do So Well

Being a single father is a nontraditional role. As such, it is interesting to consider why the fathers in the study feel so resoundingly positive about their children (as stated, the majority were satisfied with their relationship with their children). The reasons may have to do both with why someone chose to answer the questionnaire and with the individual characteristics of the people involved. This was a self-selected group; clearly there were men in the sample who wanted to crow about how well they were doing, to share their pride with the world. Fathers also may have wanted to provide a good impression of the single father with custody in order to improve other people's view of them.

The nature of single fatherhood is also a contributing factor. For a father to have custody in the first place, he must, in most cases, have gone through a decision-making process that reflects a great deal of preparation on his part. It can be assumed that most of the fathers in this study had some choice in the matter. Only 20 percent were deserted by their wives. They had time to consider the pros and cons of raising their children. Many fathers, by their own account, wanted custody very much; some had to go out of their way to get it. The fact that the fathers wanted their children and worked hard for them (even though they were bucking tradition by getting them) may compensate for an anticipated lack of satisfaction with their children and themselves. In other words, because these fathers went against the grain to get their children, they may have gained a more positive outlook on parenting.

The strong desire of these men to raise their children makes them work harder as parents. It makes them try harder to establish a good relationship with the children. That desire also may make them a little blind when it comes to objectively assessing their children's progress. Such a task is difficult for all parents who want to believe their children are doing well. For the single father who has sought out this nontraditional role, the belief may be especially strong, as is his desire to make it true.

The desire to make things work may also exist from the children's perspective. Ambert (1982, 1984), after studying a small sample of single mothers and fathers with custody, was left with the impression that the children of single fathers heard a lot about how wonderful their father was because he was raising them alone. This feedback, Ambert believes, made the children feel special and made them try harder to make things work than children raised by their mothers did.

The father may also believe his children are progressing well because they may have escaped a bad situation at home that is alleviated by the absence of the mother. Living with him, following a volatile marital relationship or desertion, might be seen as a relief from years of fighting. The father sees himself as providing an oasis for the children, so he assumes the children will do better than they had been doing.

The father may give himself a good rating as a parent for many of the reasons mentioned already: He worked hard to obtain them; he receives positive feedback from some people because he has them; his children are working at the relationship and feel special. He is also comparing himself to his ex-wife, whom both society and the children may view negatively. He is often more willing to vocalize his negative feelings than are mothers. DeFrain and Eirick (1981) compared the life-styles of single mothers and single fathers with custody; the only difference they found was in the amount of negative criticism voiced by the parents. Fathers shared many more negative comments about their noncustodial ex-wives than single mothers shared about their noncustodial ex-husbands.

Almost all the fathers interviewed in this study denied talking negatively about their ex-wives. They held the relationship between themselves and their children and that between their children and their ex-wives as sacred, and claimed to discourage negative comments. One California policeman who was raising a teenaged son and daughter said: "To help my children adjust, I never said anything negative about their mother. They had to form an opinion about it. When they brought things up, they were negative. I said, 'Well, she is your mother and you have to be respectful of her.'"

This prevailing view of the mother as a bad parent (discussed in depth in chapter 8) may save the children from the fathers' bad feelings; but it has the reverse effect on the father, who sees himself more positively by comparison. He may rate himself highly as a parent in part because the other parent he has seen up close, his ex-wife, is viewed negatively. For these reasons, it is evident why the fathers tend to be satisfied with themselves as parents and with how their children are doing. As in any family, however, what the children are experiencing is also key to understanding the father-child relationship.

## The Child's Part

Children coping with divorce can be expected to have problems. The breakup of the family is a serious, traumatic event for all involved. Simultaneously, the children have to adjust to a new family situation. Children, depending on their age, their past and present relationship with their parents, their support systems, their self-image, and a number of other factors, have a range of reactions. Children in the same family often adjust differently to a divorce. The toll the divorce takes on one child, as in Charlie's situation, may differ from its effect on another. In fact, it is rare for the reactions of different children in the same family to be similar. This also means the satisfaction the father may feel with his children's progress will vary from child to child. Although there may be a good deal of general satisfaction on the father's part, there are also problems. Peter, for example, was probably more satisfied with Susan's progress than the progress of Keith, Vince, and Barry.

The policeman quoted earlier is pleased with his son's progress but not with his daughter's: "They [the children] have adjusted well to living with me. They were, at first, surprised by our breakup [two years ago], but after six months, they adjusted to it. Grades have been up and down. My son's are up and my daughter's down. She is having a problem with one of the teachers in school and is starting to date, and adolescence is quite a thing to go through." In this situation, the particular age of the child is also taking its toll.

A factory worker from Indiana with four children has also had problems with one of his children, some of which he believes are exacerbated by his ex-wife. "The children were very upset with the divorce. My oldest daughter is having a big problem. She thought her mother would change her mind and come back. When problems came up between her and her mother, they became my problems too. I got my daughter [age eighteen] a job. She got fired. She doesn't want to do anything. I helped her get a car, and now I am making the payments. She has kind of dropped out. I tried to get her help; she refuses. She's a good girl around the house, but she just dropped out. She said she will get herself straightened out, but I think I am going to get professional help. The other children are doing great. I had to change everything around to get things done in the home. I was very involved with the children."

A third father, a biologist from New York whose ex-wife visits once a week, is raising three children. He describes great differences in the adjustment of the children. He tells how he pulled the wool over his own eyes in an attempt to give himself a better impression of his children: "Each child reacted differently. They are still paying the price. The oldest pulled into herself and still is. The middle became unhappy and would cry. I would get in touch with his mother and that would help. The youngest had it the hardest. He was six and now has a hard time dealing with women. The more assertive his mother was, the more he fought her. They seemed to have recovered, and I thought it was just me having problems, and I was wrong. They all were, too. I wanted to see them doing well."

What these three fathers have in common they share with many of the other fathers: variation in how their children are doing. When questioned closely during interviews, however, many of the fathers who report problems see the situation either as an improvement over what the children had been going through or as an improvement over what they would be going through if they were living with their mother. For many fathers, this becomes a recurring theme: The children are doing well given the circumstances.

## Characteristics of the Children

Many parents secretly—or not so secretly—admit to having an easier time being with a child of a particular age or a particular sex. The satisfaction the fathers reported with how their children were progressing since living with them, and the satisfaction they felt with their relationship with their children, also varied based on the age and sex of the children they were raising.

### Age of the Children

Because fathers are traditionally less involved in the upbringing of younger children than of older children, it was believed that the fathers raising younger children would have the least satisfaction. This did not prove to be the case. The older the children being raised, the less satisfaction there was in the father's relationship with the children and in how he saw the children progressing. In both instances, fathers raising children in the one- to four-year-old range had the most satisfaction. Fathers raising twelve- to eighteen-year-olds experienced the least.

Other differences relating to the greater ease of raising younger children were found. For example, there was a tendency for fathers to give themselves higher ratings as parents if they were raising younger children. In addition, fathers who were raising younger children found their children's feelings less difficult to handle: Almost one-fifth of the fathers raising the youngest children reported difficulty in this area, compared with approximately one-third of the fathers raising five- to eleven-year-olds and one-half of the fathers raising the oldest children. The age of the children being raised influenced the comfort the fathers felt in disciplining the children and doing activities with them. Again, the younger the children, the greater comfort the father felt.

On one level, these findings are not surprising. Anyone who has been around teenagers knows they can be difficult to raise. The issues teens present to parents are much more crucial than those posed by a younger child. Worrying about a fifteen-year-old's sexual and drug experimentation has helped sprout many gray hairs. In addition, school performance as it relates to career and college plans becomes one more area of concern. With a younger child, there is obviously more time spent in child care, but probably less sleep lost in worrying. There is also more control over younger children, as they are less independent. A father can order a disobedient five-year-old to his room. A fifteen-year-old cannot be handled in the same way.

There are other factors that may account for the greater satisfaction in raising younger children. With the loss of daily contact with the mother, an older child may turn to peer groups for support; a younger child, lacking that option, may turn to the father. For some men, this can provide a feeling of being needed that results in greater satisfaction. It also brings the parent and child closer.

Many teens also are better able to make contact independently with the noncustodial mother, which may stir up emotions in the father and affect his relationship with that child. The younger child's contact with the mother can be more easily filtered or controlled.

Because the father spends more time with younger children and they rely on him more, it is easier to establish the classic parent–child relationship, where there is dependence on the parent. The father spends less time with his children as they age; and, as the children develop, their relationship with their father changes. The father is not needed in the same way. For some fathers, the disruption of their families and not being needed in the way they used to be can be another source of stress that reduces satisfaction in the parental relationship.

Younger children may also be easier because they may have an easier time adjusting than older children. Wallerstein (1984) reported that children who were very young at the time of the breakup had a rougher initial period but seemed to be better off after a few years than children who were older when their parents split up.

On a different level, these findings are surprising. Fathers traditionally have been more involved with their children as they get older and have left the child-care duties of the very young to their wives. It would be expected, then, that they would feel more capable of dealing with the demands of parenting older children than younger children. For years this expectation has guided the courts in cases of disputed custody.[5] Clearly this has changed recently, but much of that thinking lingers and has had some effect on the fathers in this study (see chapter 9 on the legal system and the father). The bias toward the mother as the most fit parent of younger children was demonstrated in this study. Fathers tend to raise the older children in arrangements in which the ex-wife has retained custody of at least one child. Yet the fathers in this study refute the myth regarding their capabilities raising younger children; they have an easier time with them than with older children.

If fathers feel more comfortable with younger children, why do they tend to raise older ones? It is not only the judge who influences the age of the children the father is raising. There has been collusion among the parties involved. The father may concur in the belief that he is less capable of raising younger children. This belief would discourage him from seeking custody in the first place. In addition, the mother may be more reluctant to relinquish custody of younger children. Unfortunately, as dubiously acceptable in the eyes of society as it is for a mother not to have custody of an older child, whom she can always describe as too hard to handle and in need of a man's firm hand, it is even less acceptable for a mother to be separated from a very young child. She can give no comparable excuse. The judge's opinion, the father's belief about his own capabilities, the tender-years presumption, and the lack of social acceptance experienced by the mother who gives up a younger child all combine to make it more likely for the father to be raising older children. Yet the findings of this survey indicate that fathers feel more comfortable with younger children. This is not to imply that fathers should not be considered suitable to raise older children. It is meant to point out the effects of this particular myth about fathers—a myth that affects both single and married fathers. Mothers, fathers, and children will ultimately benefit from three major ramifications that are involved in dispelling this myth.

1. If men realize that fathers raising children alone feel more comfortable with younger children, it may encourage them to become more involved with younger children in the intact family than they traditionally have been.
2. This finding will encourage fathers to seek custody if there is a divorce. They will not be scared off by the age of their children.
3. Mothers will learn that the father is capable of feeling comfortable raising younger children and that she does not have to retain custody solely because of the child's age and the stigma that will follow if she gives up custody.

## Sex of the Children Being Raised

"I keep wondering if there is some secret I don't know about raising girls," stated a father who had been raising a three-year-old girl alone for six months.

Just as the age of the child has been a factor in the judge's and the parents' deciding on custody, so has the sex of the child.[6] Mothers have been more likely to get daughters and fathers to get sons because of the belief that a child is better off with the parent of the same sex as a role model. Much of the research on children has shown that a child of a divorced family fares better when being raised by the same-sex parent.[7] The tendency for a child to be raised by the same-sex parent was found in this study also. The fathers were raising four boys to every three girls; and, among the children living elsewhere, there were three girls to every two boys.

It was surprising, then, that fathers raising only boys and fathers raising only girls did not differ in the amount of satisfaction they felt with their relationship with their children, in how the children were doing, or in the rating they gave themselves as parents. Nor did differences appear between groups in the difficulty the fathers experienced in handling the feelings of boys and girls, or in the ease the fathers felt in disciplining and doing activities with the children.

Other differences did appear. In a number of ways, the fathers found women more important to their daughters than their sons. For example, half of the fathers raising only girls, as compared with one-third of the fathers raising only boys, believed that a woman, rather than a man, should be doing some of the things with the children that he was doing. Similarly, two-thirds of the fathers raising girls, as compared with one-half the fathers raising boys, had found it helpful to have a woman spend time with their children. These fathers tend to feel that the needs of daughters are different from those of sons and that female role models can play a more important part in their daughters' adjustment than in that of their sons. One impression gained by talking with fathers was that they worried more about their daughters than about their sons. Involving other women in their daughters' lives was one way of coping with that worry, which usually revolved around having a role model available.

How does the use of other women come into play? One Philadelphia father talked about the help he received from the neighborhood in getting his daughter ready for her first high school prom. With his son, he had handled everything himself. Many fathers talk about asking women they know to discuss sexuality and feminine hygiene with their daughters. These issues do not mean the father is less satisfied with his relationship with his daughter than with his son. These are differences in parenting—in what the father has to do to raise a daughter or a son. These differences may cause him more concern and make the father work harder to meet the needs of a daughter, but they do not necessarily have a negative impact on his handling of the child's feelings, on his closeness to the child, or on his feelings about how a daughter is progressing emotionally compared with a son.

Interviews conducted with both the fathers and the children (see chapter 11) provide further support for the contention made here and elsewhere that fathers face a different set of tasks when raising daughters than sons. A number of anecdotal findings emerged. One is that daughters may vie for fathers' attention and affection more than sons do. One father, who has been raising two sons aged ten and fourteen and a seventeen-year-old daughter, made this point clearly: "My daughter never approved of any of the dates [I had], probably because she did not want someone replacing her mother. Maybe she was jealous." It is difficult to imagine a father thinking his son was jealous.

Another father said, "My daughters are more interested in who I date than my son. That's just girls." Certainly we see this in Peter and Susan's relationship, too.

Fathers are aware of these differences in sex-role behavior. Some men find them amusing. Laughingly, one father told of lying to his daughter—saying he was going bowling when he really had a date. These differences do not affect the quality of the relationship between father and daughter unless the daughter's behavior reaches an extreme point, as it has in a few cases. In those situations, fathers have described their daughters as being withdrawn or depressed when the father dated. Sometimes a daughter has put up vehement opposition to the father's dating that he considered extreme.

Not only are daughters likely to be more jealous of the father dating than are sons, they are also likely to want to see more of their mother. As discussed in chapter 8, daughters do have more contact with their mothers than sons do. This desire or need for contact with the mother may place a strain on a daughter-father relationship if the father thinks he is not being appreciated or if the daughter expresses a desire to live with her mother.

Situations that cause problems for both daughter and father arise when the daughter becomes the so-called parentified child. The *parentified child* is the child who, in the absence of a second parent in the home, assumes some of the responsibilities the missing parent once fulfilled. In a single-father-headed family, the tendency is for a daughter to try to take the place of a missing mother. The daughter, usually the oldest child or the oldest girl in the home, may start to act like a mother hen toward the younger children. She may also take over the cooking and cleaning, and become the father's confidant. Tracy in chapter 11 and Susan in chapter 2 are two examples of this. This responsibility robs the daughter of her own peer-related activities and can also cause friction in the household. Some fathers have had housekeepers quit because the daughters were interfering with their work. In large families, this situation can work out to everyone's benefit and assure the smooth running of the household while the father works. If the child is overburdened, however, or is parenting the younger children inadequately, problems can occur.

Larry gives one example. Since he and his wife separated, he has been raising a teenaged daughter and two younger sons. His daughter, Judy, began taking the two boys places the mother used to take them—the zoo, the park, the ice cream store. Larry was happy with this arrangement because it kept his sons happy. But when Judy began doing the cooking, too, her grades suffered. Only when an astute teacher pointed out to Larry what was going on did he relieve Judy of her parenting duties. He still subtly encourages Judy to take over, however, because it makes things easier for him.

There are also a number of situations in which the son has been described as more difficult to raise. Some fathers told of great conflicts between "two strong male personalities" in the home. These fathers and sons are depicted as constantly at loggerheads without a woman to defuse their conflict. The sons may refuse to help out at home, making the father's chores more burdensome. Not having a woman around the house has made it difficult for some of the sons to get along with women outside the home as well.

On the positive side—and this is where the balance comes in—many fathers talked about the warm feelings generated between themselves and their daughters. One father wrote: "My daughter can wrap me around her finger. We have a special understanding that I don't think I would have if I had a boy."

These findings suggest a number of things. First, from the father's perspective, fathers feel as satisfied with their relationship with their children, with how their children are progressing, and with themselves as parents whether they are raising boys or girls. Second, however, the father does feel less comfortable in his role, and does value the input of women more, if he is raising girls. Third, daughters require more work for the father to raise than sons because there is more the fathers claim to not know and a greater need for female role models.

Daughters are harder to raise than sons in some cases, but this does not seem to affect the satisfaction the fathers have in their relationships with their daughters.

## Conclusions

Most fathers feel very satisfied with their relationship with their children and with how their children are progressing. From their own point of view, fathers make good parents. They also feel comfortable disciplining their children and doing activities with them, both areas in which many of these fathers had been involved during the marriage.

Implications for disputed custody cases emerge when the age of the children is looked at in light of the father's satisfaction. Fathers raising older children feel less satisfied with their relationship with their children and with a number of related areas than do fathers raising younger children. This may indicate that the fathers should not be excluded from consideration as sole custodians simply because of the myth that fathers cannot raise young children. In fact, they feel *more* comfortable with younger children. This same myth includes the belief that fathers are more capable than mothers of raising older children. Such thinking continues the stereotyping that damages the understanding of single mothers and single fathers. It relegates mothers to the role of caretaker of the young and excludes fathers, in both the intact and the divorced family, from feeling competent with small children.

It was also found that fathers do not feel less satisfaction in their relationships with sons than with daughters. The quality of the relationship is different, though. Daughters cause the fathers more concerns. Parenting them appears to require more work than parenting sons. Studies of children have established that children fare better with the same-sex parent in a single-parent family. The findings of this study indicate that the father would partially agree.

It may be useful to conceptualize much of the previous discussion systemically. Each person in a family has an effect on another family member. We know that the way a parent copes with divorce usually affects how the children will cope. If the single father is doing well, the children he is raising will probably do well. The reverse may also be true. This may be an important variable in the discussion. More research is needed. Isolating selected variables cannot always give a true picture. But it is clear that fathers, mothers, and judges should not exclude the father from consideration as a sole parent based only on the age of the children. If parents cannot share custody in some form, an attempt should be made to find the best fit between the needs of the child and the capabilities of the parent.

# 7
# Adjusting to Being Single Again

I usually date frequently, but I have been involved with one woman now for a few months. I only bring home dates after I have been dating them for a while and only if they are decent, nice people so the kids make a nice friend. The kids are battle-scarred veterans because they have seen women come and go, which can be good and bad because they may think women come and go all of the time. [The father is raising three sons.] They make comments as to my taste. The person I am now dating gets high marks. They sometimes spot problems before I do. A woman I dated for a very long time, they kept telling me that she did not like them and that she was competing with them for me. I ignored them for the longest time. I don't let them decide who I date but when we broke up, that was one of the reasons."

For the single father raising children alone, much more is involved than just the adjustments necessary to running a household, arranging school and work schedules, and raising the children. There is also the adjustment to being single again. The father must begin to feel comfortable as a single person whose marriage has ended. He must deal with loneliness. He must adjust to doing some of the things with his children that his wife may have been doing and that men traditionally have not done. Finally, to complete the adjustment process, at some point he must begin to date.

The fathers in this study found these issues among the hardest to handle. The experiences reported show a wide variation. Some fathers date frequently and describe very satisfying social lives; others almost never go out and wonder how other single fathers find the time and the money. Loneliness is one of the most difficult problems for many of the fathers. Overall, when compared with the fathers' experiences with the other demands of parenting, they are less comfortable about being single again and socializing than in any other area of their lives.

Until recently the research on fathers treated their social lives casually. There are two reasons for this. The first is related to the great interest in children. Fathers with custody tend to focus on their parenting abilities while ignoring other facets of their lives. The second reason is that research tends to focus on problem areas, and the stereotype of single men in our society has been that they do not have social problems. Generally, men are thought to be in the driver's seat when it comes to socializing. Most people believe that men have permission to initiate dating and to have sexual relations without commitment. This view can be brought into sharper focus when contrasted with the lack of societal permission granted women—especially single mothers—to initiate dating or to engage in sexual relations.

These commonly held beliefs about men include some holdovers from the past. Men can be aggressive and assertive, and they can have sexual relations without guilt. They can be content staying single, and they can be carefree about their involvements. As the fathers in this study relate their feelings about being stereotyped, however, the inaccuracies and the harm caused by viewing men in these ways become apparent. Many men, rather than seeing these myths as permissive, feel they are restrictive. The myths put pressure on the men to perform. Men react by feeling they are not supposed to get too deeply involved. They begin to treat women as sex objects and turn to other men for intellectual stimulation. Some men become suspicious of involvement, believing their feelings are not understood.

What happens to a man socially after a divorce is the result of a number of past factors, current conditions, and future hopes. The father's reaction to the divorce can vary from elation to severe depression, depending on the individual and the circumstances surrounding the marriage. Much has been written about the social adjustments that face separated and divorced people. The breakup can give rise to emotional and physical ailments and to feelings of disorientation, loss, and guilt.[1] Adjusting to the divorce means accepting the end of the dream of a happy married life and reassessing one's values and goals. For many men, adjusting to the loss of both a marriage and the companionship of a once-loved woman can be extremely painful and may take years to overcome.

When children are present, a new set of stresses is involved. The parents have to deal not only with their own adjustment but also with their children's adjustment and the barriers to socializing that the children may throw in their way. This adds to the parent's sense of failure and makes the loss of the dream of the happily married family more wrenching.

The research on single fathers varies in its conclusions about how fathers adjust socially. Some studies conclude that fathers have problems dating and feeling comfortable being single; others do not report this as a problem area. Many studies report that the fathers were not anxious to remarry, because they either were satisfied with their lives, were wary of new relationships, or did not want to upset the children.[2]

## The Fathers in This Study

Adjusting to being single again proved to be one of the greatest areas of difficulty for the fathers in this study. Only 37 percent indicated that they felt satisfied with their social lives, whereas 38 percent had mixed reactions and 25 percent were unsatisfied with their social lives. Fewer than half agreed with the statement, "I feel comfortable being single again."

The fathers in this study, of course, may be different from fathers who are not members of Parents Without Partners in ways that are incalculable. It could be argued that because they joined PWP, they have more active social lives than do fathers who have not. To the contrary, it could be argued that they did not have active social lives and therefore joined PWP to take advantage of its educational and social benefits for themselves and their children. They may have stayed with the organization because of a continued lack of fulfillment or because their needs were being met. It is important to keep these sampling differences in mind when discussing the findings.[3]

## The Fathers' Social Lives

The fathers in this study led fairly active social lives. The responses on the questionnaire give an overview of the frequency of dating as well as the people with whom the fathers socialize. Almost half reported dating at least once a week, and another quarter dated once or twice a month. Only one in twenty indicated they never dated. The people seen most frequently by the fathers are women they are dating and other single parents.

These fathers also maintain social lives with their children. More than three-quarters of the fathers socialize at least once a month with their children; half of them socialize with their children at least once a week.

The people with whom the single-father family socializes are, as expected, different from those the father sees when he socializes without his children. Seen most frequently with the children are relatives, whom the father does not see nearly as much on his own. Single-parent families and two-parent families are seen next most frequently, followed by friends of the children. Relatives are most likely seen the most often because they can help the family hold onto some of the ties that existed when the mother was still present. Relatives supply continuity, love, and a feeling of belonging that the family may need more acutely after the breakup.

## The Fathers' Social Satisfaction

Despite their relatively active social lives, these fathers do not report a great deal of satisfaction. Only about one-third said they were socially satisfied.

A range of reasons have been given for fathers' lack of pleasure with their social lives. We know the pain of divorce can be a great deterrent to enjoying the company of a date. The majority of the fathers in this study did not want the marriage to end, and another portion were unsure whether they wanted it to end. Not only did most men not want the marriage to end, but three-quarters of them indicated they experienced a great deal of stress when it did.

Another one-fifth said they experienced some stress. Perhaps contributing to their stress was the nature of the breakup: Nearly half the men said the breakup came as a surprise.

Reentering the social scene following an unwanted and perhaps unexpected marital breakup can contribute to difficulties in adjusting to being single and to dating. These fathers had little or no time for preparation, and they did not have the luxury of choosing their single status.

For these reasons, many of the fathers are wary of new relationships, both because of the pain they have experienced and also because of potential conflicts with their children. Fathers expressed feelings of guilt at having the marriage fail and seeing the difficulties the children experienced because of the divorce. As long as their children seem emotionally vulnerable, many men want to maintain the stability they have established in the home. A new relationship or a new wife would threaten the stability that many men have worked so hard to achieve. It is this commitment to making things right for their children that leads some men to avoid involvement.

The result of this commitment is that some of these men have put their children's well-being first, to the exclusion of their own. One custodial father from Wisconsin, raising two young daughters, said what many others also think: that his children come first and his social life second. For him, dating had been infrequent because he believed it took something away from his children.

The pain of the marital breakup and worries about new relationships are not these men's only problems. If they finally do begin dating, they may experience culture shock. The median year of divorce for the fathers in the study was 1978, following an average of twelve years of marriage. When these fathers left the social scene as single men to get married in the mid-1960s, expectations of men and women were very different from current ones. At that time, a man was expected to initiate dating and be sexually aggressive. By the time these men began dating again, much had changed. Sexual contact without emotional commitment had become more acceptable for women. Women were becoming more sexually aggressive. Men, in turn, were becoming less assertive and more nurturing. The role of the so-called new man was creeping into the culture.

For many fathers, these changes placed incredible demands on them, even though the thrust of the role change was intended to be liberating. One fifty-five-year-old father, a lawyer in a rural town, described being single again after thirty years of marriage: "Men and women are not the same as they were when I was first married. Women who believe in old-fashioned values are hard to find." The woman with old-fashioned values is the kind of woman he married in 1950 and the kind of woman is he looking for now.

When the men begin to date, more than these changes in dating behavior must be faced; there is also a lack of money. Many men expressed the feeling that because of the costs of parenting, they could not date in the way they wanted to. They cannot go out to nice restaurants or to shows as they did when they were last single. For some men, this is an emasculating experience that inhibits their desire to date.

The more comfortable a father was financially, the more he dated. The fathers in the survey had an average income of $28,000, which for some men was adequate enough for them to pursue an active social life. The less a father earned, the more difficult it became. One father, reading in the PWP magazine, *The Single Parent*, about some of the findings from this study, wrote to me about the extreme difficulties his lack of money had caused him: "I joined the local PWP chapter and did not even have the money to buy a suit to wear. Your article talks about *Kramer vs. Kramer*, and let me tell you that guy had it damned good." Another man said he had not gone out on dates because he only had enough money to make ends meet for himself and his children. The luxury of dating was something he could not afford.

For fathers who wish to bring dates home, there are additional hurdles. It is difficult to have a romantic dinner in one room while the children are making popcorn and watching "Dallas" in another. Many fathers do not have their dates sleep over because they do not want to cause more turmoil for the children. As one North Carolina father, who was raising three small children, put it: "The kids have been confused enough by the divorce. I don't want to confuse them any more."

A Michigan father gave a different reason for not bringing dates home—one that for some fathers is even more important. He told this story: "I was able to get custody from my wife because she violated the court order by being immoral and having guys sleep over. I know she is waiting to catch me do the same thing."

Despite the natural concerns of not wanting to upset the children by dating and not wanting to "confuse" them by having dates sleep over, some fathers do finally allow their children to meet the women for whom they have more serious feelings. Usually this happens when the father believes his relationship has reached a point at which a long-term commitment is being considered. The woman may begin to spend more time with the children, including sleeping at the father's home. Some fathers talk to the children first about the woman in order to get their reactions. Many fathers have good ideas about their children's impressions, as the children may have been offering an unsolicited commentary on the woman during the initial period of the relationship. The father may float a trial balloon of marriage past the children to get their reactions to the idea.[4]

As with all aspects of the father's dating, this can be a difficult time for the child, and fathers are quick to sense it. Some children welcome the relationship; others express great concern. For the child who has clung to the hope of seeing his or her parents reunited, meeting a more permanent replacement for their mother (or even seeing their father casually dating) can be devastating. It forces the child to face what many children have difficulty accepting: that family life as they knew it when the parents were married will never return. The dream dies for the child just as it did for the father when the marriage ended. The average father in the study had his first serious intimate relationship about 3.5 years after the breakup. This period of time often gives the child a chance to adjust to the breakup. For many of the children, however, there would never be enough time. Some of the varying reactions to dating and remarriage are pointed out by Peter and Gail's children.

It is not only the father's feelings and the children's reactions that make dating difficult. Another factor for many of these men is the reaction of the women they are dating. The woman involved with a single father finds herself confronted with a number of obstacles and questions. She may be unsure whether she is desirable because she would make a good wife for the father, a good mother for the children, or simply a good companion. Attempts to clarify this with the father may be futile, as he may be unsure about his own needs at the moment. Some women have stayed involved with the father for many years, hoping that as the children age, the father's commitment to them may change and permit him to make a place for her in his life. Sometimes this is the case, but in other situations women give up hope and flee. Other women, spotting potential quicksand, avoid serious involvements with fathers who, they perceive, must put their children first. The woman's uncertainty about where she stands causes greater stress for all involved and may make the father shy away from other relationships for a while.

Some fathers also feel that women are not really interested in raising his children. These women either may have children of their own and not want to blend families, or may be scared off by the added responsibility of the father's children. The father quoted at the beginning of this chapter said: "Some of my relationships have ended because of this. It raises the questions about how single parents are willing to deal with another single parent's children."

Finally, the role of the ex-wife must be considered. Her involvement with the children and the father affects the way the children view the father's dating. Usually one of two possible reactions is caused by the mother's involvement. If the mother maintains contact with the children and the father, the children may be encouraged to believe their parents are going to reconcile. The children would then discourage the father from dating. Some children, however, if the mother maintains contact, feel secure enough to believe that, regardless of what happens with their father, they will always have a stable relationship with their mother. Here, dating poses no threat.

Two opposing reactions also occur when the mother is not involved. If the mother is not involved with the children, the father's dating holds open the door for a new mother, and may be encouraged for that reason. On the other hand, without much contact with their mother, the children sometimes become too much invested in their father. In that case, his dating poses the threat of diverting his attention from them to someone new.

## Who Is the Most Satisfied Socially?

Fathers who earn more money and are raising older children tend to be the most socially satisfied. The reasons are clear. Money gives the father more opportunity to date the way he wants to. Older children make fewer demands on the father because they require less physical care and are more apt to have their own social life. In addition, fathers with older children are likely to have been single longer, giving them more time to adjust. In summary, the following points can be made:

1. Most fathers did not initiate the breakup, nor did they wish to be single.
2. Fathers do tend to lead active social lives.
3. However, they are not particularly satisfied with their social lives.
4. The more money they make and the older their children, the more apt they are to enjoy socializing.

## Adjusting to Being Single

Dating is only part of the adjustment a father makes to being single again. A number of other feelings and transitions must be handled when a father's marriage has ended and he has custody. He has to begin adapting to a number of different roles. He has to start wearing the hat of a divorced person as well as the hat of a father in a nontraditional role. Each of these hats can be a thorny crown. Wearing them both pulls on different emotions in the fathers. Comfort in these areas is achieved by dealing with the feelings of loneliness that follow a marital split, being accepted by society as a single parent, and doing some of the things with their children that a mother traditionally has done.

These psychological adjustments are often harder for men to make than the more concrete adjustments of running a household or setting up a child-care schedule. Slightly fewer than half of the fathers felt comfortable being single again.

Part of the difficulty for some of these fathers is that they are seen as being extraordinary people. Because they are raising their children, they are viewed as being exceptionally caring men. They are treated more deferentially than single mothers with custody and than single fathers and mothers without custody. Because they are put on a pedestal, their needs are not seen realistically. Some fathers like this special treatment; others do not.

The father quoted at the beginning of this chapter talks about his reaction to the special treatment he gets because he is a single father: "I have learned how to use my status to my advantage. I walk into stores for help with clothing and the saleswomen rush to help. I would tell them I needed help in dressing my three boys and they would do all of the work. They saw me as being noble and thought my wife was terrible. I needed everything I could get. There was sympathy for this great man."

A number of fathers interviewed appreciated the help they received, because it meant less work for them. There can be problems with this treatment, however. One father, telling his story at a workshop for custodial fathers, speaks of his discomfort: "I just want to be treated normally. I don't like when people gush all over me because I have my kids. It isn't fair. It isn't me."

Not all fathers are put on a pedestal. A few had indicated they feel uncomfortable because people have implied they are deviant or sick. These fathers have problems getting sitters because teenaged girls—or their parents—do not consider it safe to come into a home in which there is no mother. Others report more extreme reactions.

A father from Ohio wrote: "My little girl came home from school last year and told me her teacher said fathers shouldn't raise little girls, that single fathers are all animals. Or how about the broad next door asking if I am sleeping with my girl or not."

For many fathers, then, the attention feels uncomfortable. It may feel uncomfortable because they are not at ease with themselves as a single parent. Having attention brought to their status as a parent means being made aware of some of their own shortcomings. Still others resent the assumption that they cannot raise their children on their own. To them, attempts to help them are insulting. Just as some women become insulted when men open doors for them, some fathers resent the similar implication that they need special treatment because of their sex.

For all fathers, whether they are comfortable with it or not, the special treatment means they are not being viewed realistically. Myths about their abilities are affecting the way people react to them.

Among these fathers, there are certain characteristics that, when present, do contribute to their feeling more comfortable being single again. Even though these will be discussed separately, the characteristics are conceptually linked.

## Who Feels Comfortable Being Single?

Those fathers who feel most comfortable being single again tend to place the responsibility for the marital breakup on incompatibility, a reason they share with their ex-wives. The reasons these fathers gave for their divorces were "we fell out of love," "we grew apart," and "we had communication problems." On the other hand, fathers who blamed their breakup on the ex-wife's infidelity or their ex-wife's leaving had a harder time adjusting to being single.

Men who feel rejected by their wives and men who blame their ex-wives' behavior for the breakup (often the same fathers) have more difficulty adjusting to being single. They have left a marriage feeling unsure of themselves, angry at their ex-wives, and angry at women in general. They may be psychologically scarred and unwilling to get involved again.

These men are also less well prepared emotionally for being single than are the fathers who initiated the divorce and those who saw the problems in the marriage as being part of the relationship. They do not like the role of single father as much and may have assumed it, in part, either to get back at their wives or because they thought their ex-wives were not competent parents because of the women's marital infidelity. These men become single fathers feeling uncomfortable from the beginning—a different situation from that of the fathers who did not leave the marriage feeling cheated or under a great deal of stress.

The fathers who wanted custody of their children, the group Mendes (1976a) calls the "seekers," also felt more comfortable being single again than did the fathers who did not want custody (the "assenters"). The seekers are better prepared for the role of father and more willing to take it on. Because of their desire for the role of single father with custody, adjustment is easier for them.

Money and time both had an impact on the father's feeling comfortable being single. The higher the income and the more years the father has had sole custody, the greater the comfort he feels being single again.

Fathers with more money may be men who, in general, feel better about themselves because of their income. Their greater financial status buys them services such as sitters and housekeepers that make dating easier. Also, to some extent, it may buy them greater confidence in themselves, as they will have more options.

Time would be expected to be linked to greater comfort, as people tend to adjust to their situations the longer they remain in them. The average father in this study began to feel comfortable sometime near the end of his third year of single parenting. With time, the father can adjust to being a divorced person and can get used to doing some of the things his ex-wife did during the marriage. His role may seem less nontraditional to him as he meets more men who are also single parents. He also is more likely to have joined a self-help group such as Parents Without Partners, which helped many fathers adjust. Housework and other home-related activities become easier with time, also, which helps the father feel more comfort with his status.

## Loneliness

Loneliness emerged as one of the greatest difficulties for the fathers. The loneliness the noncustodial parent feels has often been discussed. He or she has lost daily contact both with a spouse and with the children. He or she usually moves into a new home and has to make a number of adjustments in terms of neighborhood contacts, friends, and routines, all of which can contribute to loneliness and isolation.

The custodial father is not immune to such feelings of loneliness either, even though he is usually in the home and has his children for company. One father, who works as an engineer, said: "I don't mind having my wife gone. It was my idea. But I was not prepared for the loneliness. After being married for twelve years, it's tough."

Those fathers who were satisfied with their social lives were also the ones who were apt to feel comfortable being single again. There was a natural overlap in these feelings. The most common pattern found among the fathers was an initial period of discomfort followed by a slow opening up of emotions and the initiation of socializing. Men who did not leave the marriage psychologically scarred or wary of women tended to begin dating sooner and to enjoy socializing more.

One such father is Mark, an account executive in his forties who is raising one son. He believes he has not been "burned" so badly by his first marriage that he would never remarry. He dates at least once a week, and he and his son take an annual ski trip with a woman he has been dating for two years. She is also a single parent with custody. Mark initiated his divorce and was sure enough of himself to begin dating soon after the breakup.

Many fathers who did not have custody when they first divorced found a real change in the way they could socialize. George, who is raising an eleven-year-old daughter while his two sons are being raised by his ex-wife, did not always have custody. At first he had freedom and then had to adjust to its loss. He says: "I go out still. I have a good social life. It used to be better. I can't run the street every night because of her. I wouldn't anyway since I am forty-six years old and I can't play that hard. I have to rest. You know you get off from work, you have to go home and be with the kid. But I still date."

Perhaps the story of Bill, a social worker, best provides a sketch of what the single father goes through socially. He and his wife broke up amicably. They are now on speaking terms but are not what he would describe as friends. He began dating three months after the breakup. When he first went out, he noticed he was choosing "safe" women—those who were not overly attractive to him or those he thought were not interested in a long-term relationship. His son, who was ten, did not express any feelings one way or the other at the time. Bill then began a serious involvement that lasted for one year. He said the relationship ended when the woman moved out of town and they decided to not get married. He then joined PWP, in part for himself and in part for his son. Currently he is one of the youngest men in his chapter and is not particularly happy socially. He says that, had he been interviewed a year earlier, when he was still involved, he would have given a much different answer. For Bill, like others, there is a slow progression to dating, often concluding in a serious relationship. Sometimes that turns into marriage. Other times it breaks up, and the father is back to square one.

## What Was Helpful

From the answers on the questionnaire, four areas emerged as being especially helpful to the fathers in adjusting to being single:

1. Meeting other single parents.
2. Getting involved in social activities.
3. Joining PWP.
4. Having an intimate relationship.

Approximately 80 percent of the men replied that they had had an intimate relationship, with nearly 80 percent of that group describing the experience as being either very helpful or somewhat helpful to their adjustment. As might be expected, the longer the father has had custody, the more likely he is to have had an intimate relationship. An intimate relationship was not further defined on the questionnaire. To some fathers it may have implied a sexual relationship, whereas to others it may have implied something else. Interestingly, the helpfulness of having a relationship goes down over time. This indicates that the intimate relationships these fathers have after the divorce are important at the time but that—in retrospect and perhaps with other experiences—their importance diminishes. Some fathers may continue their involvements but may place them in a different perspective, relying more on themselves and less on women.

Fathers were also asked to indicate what they thought would be most helpful to their adjustment. Being accepted as a single parent, along with greater legal support, was considered most important. As might be expected, fathers who did not feel comfortable being single again had a greater need to be accepted than fathers who did feel comfortable.

## Reaction of Others

The way the father feels he is treated by others plays a key part in his overall adjustment. The theme that emerges again and again is that society does not understand these men. Some fathers deal with this better than others; some receive more understanding than others. One father from San Francisco, who is raising three children under seven, said: "I haven't gotten too much overt discrimination; a little of it is covert. Some people think I am odd. One date thought I was mean to take the children away from their mother. I never know what to expect."

Another father living in Des Moines, who had had custody for less than six months, said: "I feel out of place, but it doesn't bother me. I'm on the reverse side of a lot of sexist comments. People assume if I am raising them there is a wife, or I have visitation and not custody. Once at a teacher conference the teacher wanted to wait to discuss my daughter until my wife arrived."

One father living in Cleveland thinks he has conquered much of the prejudice he initially encountered: "All my neighbors know I can do it. They have their children come over and spend the night. At first, my youngest daughter's friends' mothers and fathers said they all of a sudden couldn't stay over. I understand what the problem was. The first thing the parents would say is, 'My God, his wife left him and I don't want him doing something to my daughter.' But when they saw me during the summer take the kids to the park and sit outside in front and talk to them and talk to their parents, I had no problems. They understood. The schools have been very nice about it. I notified them. Talked to the teachers and told them about the situation in case a problem occurred there."

Some of the fathers, in their struggles to adjust, become acutely aware of the demands single parenting places on single mothers. A father from Philadelphia with three teenagers said: "I don't feel that being a single father presents any more problems than being a single mother would. Women are more adept at cleaning the house than men, but we do it even though we don't like it. Ninety percent of the women have to go out and get a job, too. At least we start with one." A father from Chicago wrote: "Take to the role of single parent. After all, we are only doing what our sisters have been doing on their own for years. And they have gotten a lot less support for it than we have."

## Conclusions

For the single father in this survey, there are a number of difficulties to overcome in establishing a social life and adjusting to being single. The men who feel the most comfortable in other areas of their parenting tend to be the ones who have the easiest time adjusting to their single status and starting social lives. These are fathers who have also given themselves permission to spend time at night away from their children. The reactions of others can go a long way toward helping or hindering the father's chances for feeling comfortable.

The myth of the father as a swinger with a different date every night does not help the father achieve comfort for himself, nor does it help people accept the single father as he really is. A more accurate and helpful picture of the single father is one that shows him experiencing loneliness, dating happily in some cases, and in other cases struggling to find himself socially.

# 8
# The Ex-Wife's Relationship with the Father and the Children

**D**oes my ex see the kids? Rarely. When we were going through all that legal stuff, though, she and her boyfriend would call and take them out for ice cream."

"They [the children] don't see her on a regular basis or talk to her on a regular basis, but during the summer they might see her if she is around."

"My only problem is trying to get a relationship started. I met a very nice woman. She can't realize why I am not ready to get married tomorrow. I told her there is still love for my ex-wife."

"I don't trust her one bit. She cost me my job and $30,000 in court costs getting the kids."

Out of all of the demands of parenting with which the single father must contend, perhaps the most important is his own and his children's relationship with his ex-wife—the mother of his children. Her involvement can be vital to the father's adjustment and to the children's happiness. If the children have a satisfactory amount of contact with their mother, their adjustment to living with their father will be smoother. In turn, the father will have an easier time raising the children and dealing with the other areas of parenting if his relationship with his ex-wife is relatively free of stress. When strain and distrust exist between the family members, life can be hell. To understand what the father has gone through, we must understand what his and the children's relationship is with the ex-wife.

Virtually everything we know about the relationship between the custodial and noncustodial parent has revolved around the reverse situation, in which the mother has the children and the father is visiting. The pictures of the visiting father in those situations usually have not been very attractive. Four of the more common ones can be described on a spectrum from worst to best.

*First picture:* The father is a ne'er-do-well who has never been involved with the children. During the marriage he was an inconsistent wage earner and a poor husband. The marriage may have ended, in part, because the wife was fed up with the way the finances were being handled and with the father's irresponsible attitude. The father may call the children only occasionally, forget their birthdays, and never visit.

*Second picture:* The father is somewhat involved with the children during the marriage and stays peripherally involved after the divorce. He misses his family and is good to the children when he is with them. His visits are infrequent, however, and he sometimes makes arrangements to see the children and then does not show up. This upsets the children greatly. He makes occasional support payments.

*Third picture:* The father was very involved with the children during the marriage, always playing the good guy. After the divorce, he takes the children on weekends and spoils them unmercifully. He becomes a weekend Santa Claus in an attempt to work off his guilt. He stimulates the children greatly by promising the moon, and leaves them drained and cranky at their mother's doorstep Sunday night. The mother picks up the pieces but finds her attempts at discipline futile after their father has allowed them enormous freedom. He usually makes his support payments but occasionally questions her about how the money is spent.

*Fourth picture:* The father was very involved with the children during the marriage. He exemplified the new man, being nurturing and sharing in the child care. After the breakup he stays involved with the children on a regular basis and pays an adequate amount of child support that has been worked out either between the mother and father or through the courts. The father and mother are on decent terms and discuss any major decisions that have to be made concerning the children.

These four pictures are broad stereotypes of the visiting father that have existed as part of our culture for years. When we think about the reverse situation—a visiting mother and a custodial father—there is no such wealth of images. Because it is unusual for a mother not to have her children following a marital breakup, a number of myths about her are constructed instead. These myths, like those about the single father with custody, are dichotomous. People often assume there is something wrong with the mother who does not have custody, as otherwise she would be raising the children. She is viewed as being unfit either because of mental problems, health problems (drug or alcohol addiction), or sexual promiscuity. Society clearly holds negative views toward the noncustodial mother.[1]

At the same time that these mothers are viewed negatively, there is the assumption that they will stay more involved with their children when they are the visiting parent than fathers do when they are visiting. Because society is invested in the idea of mothers fulfilling their role as nurturers, it is assumed that they will continue in that role even when they do not have custody. The result is the picture of the noncustodial mother as being both unfit *and* very involved with her children after the breakup. As will be shown in this chapter and elsewhere in the book, this picture is not necessarily accurate. In fact, Gail, in chapter 2, is a testimony to the inaccuracy of the stereotypical unfit mother.

## Other Research on Fathers and Their Ex-Wives

The feelings that remain between spouses after they break up affect how they get along as single people. Although the anger felt after a breakup has been documented, it has also been found that people who are divorced often retain a strong attachment for each other. Weiss (1976), reports that maritally separated individuals want to rejoin their spouses and also express anger toward them: ". . . there persists after the end of most marriages, whether the marriages have been happy or unhappy, whether the disruption has been sought or not, a sense of bonding to the spouse" (p. 138). Because of these mixed feelings of anger and attachment, spouses frequently deal with their ambivalence by suppression and compartmentalization of feelings, or by alternating between expressions of positive and negative feelings. Involvement with a "significant other" often does not reduce this feeling of attachment.

Hetherington, Cox, and Cox (1976), in a study of divorced fathers, report that the attachment felt by the men in their study persisted even after the dissolution of acrimonious marriages. In fact, 12 percent of the men in their study had intercourse with their ex-spouses within two months after the divorce was finalized. This attachment, along with the negative feelings, serves to make resolution of the postmarital relationship all the more difficult. There is a pushing away and a pulling toward that may go on between ex-spouses.

When children are involved, the situation is more complex. Not only is there the marital relationship to be resolved; but the issues involving child rearing, financial support, and visitation may pose even greater impediments to dealing with the ex-spouse.

The information provided by the custodial fathers in this study in many instances supports the past research. Like the fathers in the study by Rosenthal and Keshet (1981) of custodial fathers, the fathers in this study viewed their ex-wives negatively after the breakup. As with the fathers in the study by Hetherington, Cox, and Cox (1976), a good deal of anger remained. There is a marked variation in the experiences of these fathers, their children, and the ex-wives. Feelings run the gamut from the very healthy and nurturing relationships of Jim and Alice, described later in this chapter, to the angry and distrustful relationship between Al and Bill and their ex-wives, which are also described.

## Mothers and Their Involvement

Let us first tackle the question of the mother's visitation. As reported by the fathers, there was great variation in the amount of visitation by the mothers.

An attempt was made to learn both the qualitative and the quantitative amount of involvement the mother had with the children. In one question, the fathers were asked to describe how involved the ex-wives were with the children. The majority of the fathers, 73 percent, described them as being "somewhat" or "slightly" involved with the children. Seven percent of the fathers described their ex-wives as being very involved; 20 percent described them as not being at all involved with the children. This question enabled the fathers to give an impression of the mother's involvement with the children and was meant to encompass all types of contact, including telephone contact and written correspondence.

The fathers gave a range of responses concerning their satisfaction with the involvement of the ex-wife. Forty-seven percent were satisfied with the level of involvement, 44 percent wished she were more involved, and 9 percent felt she was too involved.

The amount of satisfaction the father feels with the ex-wife's involvement depends on the particular situation. A father may be satisfied with his ex-wife's involvement even if she has no contact with the children. This situation arises when the father does not trust the mother, does not think she is a competent parent, or has other feelings about her that make it uncomfortable for him to have her visit the children. A father also may be unsatisfied if his ex-wife is very involved. In this situation the father would prefer to be left alone, for similar reasons.

The fathers, in a separate question, were asked to indicate the frequency of the ex-wife's visitation. Almost half the fathers said the ex-wives visited at least every other week, with the rest visiting less frequently, and approximately one in ten never visiting. The following table shows the responses:

### Frequency of Visitation Between Ex-Wife and Children
(Fathers could check all that applied)

Once a week or more: 24%

Every other week: 22%

Once a month: 14%

Other ("when she wants," "three, four times a year,"
  "if I send her money," etc.): 20%

Summers: 15%

Holidays: 15%

Never: 9%

Information was also gained about the number of overnight visits between the children and the ex-wife. (It should be noted again here that fathers who reported that their ex-wives saw the children for more than ten nights a month were excluded from the study.) Almost half the fathers reported that their children and ex-wives spent no overnight visits together. The average number of overnight visits the children spent with their mothers was a little less than two a month, with four being the most common number of nights spent by those who did spend nights together. Almost half the mothers were reported to visit their children at least every other week, which would indicate a fair amount of involvement on the mothers' part. When overnight visits occurred, the most common pattern would be a weekend visit every other week. Given the nature of what happens to a family after a divorce, with parents often moving far away from each other, this frequency of visitation shows that mothers do tend to stay actively involved. (This can be contrasted with the visitation pattern of noncustodial fathers, discussed in chapter 10.)

Two of the findings related to visitation need to be explored here. As might be expected, mothers were slightly more likely to visit when the father was raising only girls than when he was raising only boys. In addition, as the children got older, and over time, visitation and the number of overnights spent together became less frequent.

The reasons mothers visit daughters more frequently than sons may be related to a number of factors:

1. Girls may reach out to mothers more than sons do.
2. The mother may feel more needed by her daughters.
3. The mother may feel that her involvement is more critical to a daughter's development than to a son's.

These reasons may also be viewed as valid ones for continued contact by the mother, the father, and the judge, who all may encourage the mother's involvement with daughters. This encouragement becomes a fourth factor for continued maternal contact.

Visitation diminishes over time and as the children get older. With time, there is a greater likelihood that the mother or father will move away, either for a career change or for a new marriage. As children age, they make friends outside their family, which may reduce the need for contact. Teenagers do not like to miss high school proms or a chance to see a James Bond movie for the twenty-ninth time just because they are scheduled to have dinner with their visiting parent.

A so-called poisoning effect can also be a factor that can affect visitation over time. Fischer and Cardea (1982), in a study of noncustodial mothers, found that visitation was occasionally blocked by the father or that the father had turned the children against the mother. Noncustodial parents of both sexes often complain that the custodial parent has poisoned the children against them, making visitation more difficult because the children believe the worst about the visiting parent. Over time this can have a cumulative effect on both the children and the mother, ultimately reducing visitation.[2]

## Feelings toward the Ex-Wives

Intertwined with the visitation between the ex-wife and the children are the father's feelings toward the ex-wife. The amount of involvement the ex-wife has with the children is often linked to the father's feelings about her, just as her feelings are linked with her involvement. These feelings are colored, of course, by the experiences the father has had with the mother both during and after the marriage. Feelings between the once-married couple run the gamut from friendly to hostile. When a couple has also shared parenting roles, there is an additional basis for conflict.

The fathers were asked to check from a list those words that best described how they generally felt toward their ex-wife. The most common feeling, held by over half the fathers, is distrust. Indifference is the second most common feeling, with anger and hurt also prevalent. The feelings expressed here tend to wax and wane with the events that are currently taking place in the relationship. A father who has not heard from his ex-wife for a year may feel indifference toward her. If she comes back into town and threatens to take the father to court to change the custody arrangements, his indifference will turn quickly into distrust and anger. The responses are presented in the following table. (Fathers were permitted to check more than one response.)

*Which Words Describe What You Generally Feel About Your Ex-Wife?*

| | | | |
|---|---|---|---|
| Distrust | 52.9% | Hate | 7.6% |
| Indifference | 40.8% | Love | 5.8% |
| Anger | 27.6% | Fear | 4.1% |
| Hurt | 25.4% | Attachment | 4.0% |
| Confusion | 14.8% | Trust | 3.8% |
| Caring | 14.6% | | |

## Rating the Ex-Wife as a Mother

Fathers' experiences affect how they rate their ex-wives as mothers. As mentioned, noncustodial mothers are not seen in a very good light by society. This view is shared by many of the fathers. One father raising a twelve-year-old son who has little contact with his mother said: "I don't blame her as a person [for leaving], but I don't trust her judgment as a mother." This feeling was prevalent among the fathers. On the survey, just over half of them gave their ex-wives a rating of poor as a mother. Only one in ten thought his ex-wife was excellent or good; the rest rated them as fair or adequate.

The fathers interviewed had a litany of complaints about their ex-wives as mothers. It may be that the ratings they gave their ex-wives are affected both by the fathers' personal experiences with the mothers and by the fathers' acceptance of the prevailing negative view of noncustodial mothers. These fathers are in a unique position both to judge the ex-wives and also to hear a lot of criticism of them. Fathers hear from many sources that their ex-wives must have problems if the ex-wives are not raising the children. These same sources most likely praise the father for what he is doing. The more the father hears from others how bad his ex-wife must be, the more he may hang onto his own negative feelings about her. Every moment he spends with his children as sole custodian reinforces to a certain extent the notion that he is doing a good job and that his ex-wife is not. On some level, this must affect his view of her.

What is being said about the mother must be looked at in context. We are hearing one side of a two-sided story. These are people who have divorced each other. Fathers without custody may have similar feelings about mothers with custody. It is difficult for some fathers to separate feelings stemming from the divorce from feelings related to the mother not having custody.

The sex of the children the father is raising and the amount of visitation from the mother have an impact on the father's view of her, also. For example, fathers raising only girls give their ex-wives slightly worse ratings as mothers than did fathers raising only boys. The role a mother is supposed to take in the eyes of the father plays a part in his view of her. There is a lower regard for her if she is a noncustodial mother of daughters than of sons, as she is straying further from the role society expects her to play.

The father who reports no visitation between the mother and the children also gives the mother a lower rating than does the father who reports more frequent visitation. In turn, the father who reports that visitation between mother and child occurs once a week or more gives the mother a higher rating than those of mothers who visit less frequently.

Although negative feelings about the mother as a person and a low rating of her as a mother often went together, in a number of instances this was not the case. One father provides such an example. Even though Jerry left his marriage because of his wife's infidelity and a number of other transgressions against him, he thinks she does an adequate job as a mother. He respects some of the ways she plays with their daughter. He recognizes the difference between his feelings about her as an ex-wife and his feelings about her as a mother. Also, even though a father may distrust his ex-wife and give her a negative rating as a mother, he may see her involvement with the children as important.

One Texas father who has been raising four children for over twelve years described this situation between his children and their mother. The marriage ended when the father asked the wife to leave because she was an alcoholic. The ex-wife maintained some contact with the children for the first few years. Then a pattern developed in which she did not see the children at all for five years, although she maintained occasional telephone contact. For the two oldest children this infrequent contact presented no hardship. For the youngest two, however, it was a problem. When the children's maternal grandmother died, they all met again at the funeral. The mother was described as being very cold toward the children. Since the funeral there has not even been telephone contact. This, again, has been hard on the two youngest children, who had benefited from the infrequent phone contact they had previously enjoyed. This father, although he does not like his ex-wife or the way she manipulates their emotions, recognizes the importance of her involvement with the two youngest children.

Accompanying the negative feelings and the negative ratings reported by most fathers were responses indicating the fathers did not rely on the ex-wife for help or want much contact with her. One-third of the fathers said they would never call their ex-wives for help with the children, and almost another half said they would call only in an emergency. Only one in thirty said he called the ex-wife frequently for help. Clearly the fathers do not rely on their ex-wives. As will be shown later, however, they do often benefit from their involvement when it exists.

The fewer the number of years the father has had custody, the more he tends to consult his ex-wife. This is probably because the longer they have been raising their children alone, the more likely men are to have gained the experience and the confidence needed to do it alone. Also, as mentioned, families tend to move away from each other over time. It was the fathers who said they did not know where their ex-wives were who had had sole custody for the greatest number of years. The fathers, then, are more likely to contact their ex-wives for help at first. Those men who do not contact their ex-wives may feel that their ex-wives are not competent to help, may want to prove to the world and themselves that they can raise their children alone, or simply may not need the help.

To some fathers, the ex-wife is seen as not only being not helpful, but actually as being a hindrance to their adjustment. This was gleaned from an open-ended question on the survey that asked the fathers to identify the person who had been the most helpful to their adjustment and the person who had been the least helpful. Fewer than 1 percent of the fathers described their ex-wife as being the most helpful, and 43 percent described her as the least helpful. The reasons given most often for why the ex-wife was not helpful were:

1. The father's attempts to cope were actively impeded by her; that is, she made things difficult for him by her actions.

2. She made things difficult for him by her lack of action, that is, she gave no assistance.
3. She made things harder for the children and hence for the father, who had to help the children cope with the mother's behavior. The mother may have made things harder for the children by promising to see them and then not coming, by having no contact with them at all, or by upsetting the children by telling them things about themselves or their father that caused pain.

Most marital separations involve a great deal of anger and hurt. These feelings are reflected here in the percentage of fathers who feel their wives have been the least helpful to their adjustment. The fathers may be feeling more hurt than in most marital breakups because they may have unrealistic expectations of the mothers' continuing involvement with the children. Again, the fathers may be responding to the notion that mothers who do not have custody stay more involved than noncustodial fathers. If this is the case, any lack of involvement on their part may be interpreted more harshly than it would be if the situation were reversed and it was the man who was not very involved with the custodial mother and the children. The fathers here may be prone to describing their ex-wives as the least helpful because of society's traditional role expectations for mothers. When the mothers cannot live up to the often unrealistic role assigned to them, bad feelings ensue.

Some fathers have a sense that they and their children are better off without any contact with the ex-wife. This is a complicated issue, colored by many other factors—for instance, by feelings of anger the father may have toward her as a result of the way the marriage ended. Although a number of fathers would like the ex-wife to be more involved than she is, because she is not involved, they may have taken a defensive stance. Such a posture says: If she does not want to be involved with her children, then the children and I are better off without her.

Fathers may also not want her to be involved because they have accepted the myth that the mother should be the primary caretaker of the children. When the father ends up with custody, it changes the way he feels about her and her involvement with the children. Finally, for many fathers, life is simply easier if they have control over the situation and the ex-wife is not around. When the mother comes in and out of the children's lives, more problems exist for the father—arranging schedules, handling the children's feelings, and handling his own feelings. For many men, the less contact there is with their ex-wives, the less they have to deal with their own feelings about the divorce.

## Impact of Wife's Involvement

One of the major hypotheses explored in the study was that the more involved the ex-wife was with the children, the easier it would be for the father to adjust to raising the children alone. This was based on a number of assumptions. It was assumed that a father whose children were still seeing their mother frequently would avoid having to make many difficult parenting decisions alone. It was assumed that the ex-wife would help buy clothes for the children; discuss sexuality with the daughters; and help with finances, housekeeping advice, and child-care arrangements.

It was further believed that the mother's involvement with the children would make the children's adjustment easier. There is support for this in the research. Wallerstein and Kelly (1980) found that the more contact the children had with the noncustodial parent, the smoother their transition to the single-parent family. It was assumed, then, that if the children were seeing their mother on a regular basis, it would be beneficial both to the children and to the father. If the children were adjusting smoothly, he would have fewer emotional highs and lows to deal with. This would make it easier for him.

Support for this can also be seen with Vince, Barry, Keith, and Susan. All of them, at various stages in their lives, felt Gail was invaluable. Gail and Peter balanced each other by providing the children what the other could not. Had Gail not maintained such close contact with the children, their story would have been much different.

Fathers who described their ex-wives as being very involved with the children did have it easier in many parenting areas. Although much of this chapter has described fathers who prefer not having their ex-wives involved and fathers who give their ex-wives low ratings and express distrust and anger toward them, there was a group of fathers who did benefit from frequent contact. The mothers' involvement with the children goes hand in hand with a number of other simultaneous events and feelings. In other words, having a mother who is very involved does not just pop up out of the thin air. It flows from other events and is maintained by continued effort and good feelings. Unfortunately, only 7 percent of the mothers were described as being very involved with the children. Marked differences were found between this small group of fathers and those whose ex-wives were less involved.

First, there were differences in the reasons for the divorce. The father who shared the blame for the divorce with his ex-wife was more apt to describe her as being very involved with the children than was the father who listed the ex-wife's infidelity or the wife's leaving as the reason for the divorce. The opposite also proved true. The father whose ex-wife was not involved was more apt to blame her for the divorce. Clearly the father who shares the blame for the divorce with his ex-wife is on better terms with her and may feel more positive about her as a mother. In this situation, all the involved parties may encourage contact between the children and the mother because of the warmer feelings that exist.

Second, fathers whose ex-wives were very involved reported higher incomes. They earned an average of $6,000 more than fathers whose ex-wives were not at all involved. When there is enough money to go around, people are more likely to get along than if money is in short supply. An example of this was given by one custodial mother who was interviewed informally. She said that relations between her and her ex-husband improved dramatically as his income improved and they could afford to maintain better individual life-styles.

Third, fathers whose ex-wives were very involved with the children found their children's feelings less difficult to handle. There are two possible reasons for this:

1. The father may be receiving help from the mother.
2. The children are experiencing less emotional turmoil because their mothers are maintaining contact with them.

Finally, fathers whose ex-wives are very involved reported less difficulty working while raising the children. Most likely, these men are receiving some child-care assistance from the mother, which makes it easier for them to travel and pursue career-related goals. For the father whose ex-wife is not nearby or is not helping out, the lack of her child-care assistance means one less option for him.

In a number of areas, then, the ex-wife's involvement can make life easier for the father and, as learned from other research, easier for the children. The father whose ex-wife is very involved with her children has less of an adjustment to make than does the man who finds himself completely without her assistance. If things are going well, the father whose ex-wife is involved has a life that may more closely parallel his married life than other fathers do. His children see their mother more often, and he has her help with the day-to-day requirements of parenting. Also, this group of fathers has a situation that comes closest to being a joint custodial arrangement.

It cannot be concluded from this research, however, that joint custody offers a better solution to the divorced family than sole custody with frequent visitation does. To reach a conclusion on that issue, we would have to compare families with joint custody with families in which one parent has sole custody and the other has liberal visiting privileges. Joint custody is unfortunately not always possible when there is great acrimony. The closer the visitation pattern comes to being shared when the father has sole custody, the more likely it is that the father will have an easier time parenting alone. Every indication from research with children also supports the benefits of frequent contact between children and the noncustodial parent.[3]

## Three Families

The benefits of having a mother involved with the family are clear, though there are some fathers who would prefer much less contact for their own sake.

The experiences of three different fathers help illustrate what evolves when the father has custody and the ex-wife is very involved with the children. Within these relationships, with frequent contact, feelings between the parents can range from warm and supportive to angry and distrustful. In all three cases described here, the fathers acknowledge (to varying degrees) the importance of the mother.

Bill lives in Illinois with his four-year-old daughter, Peggy. Bill describes a stormy marital relationship that grew worse after Peggy was born. When Peggy was two, Bill believed things had reached an unbearable level between his wife and himself. His wife had physically attacked him on a number of occasions; although she had never harmed their daughter, he feared she would. He took Peggy and moved out. After many months of costly and lengthy legal battles, the custody situation was legalized.

Currently, and with court approval, Bill's ex-wife sees Peggy every day. She is very involved with the child, and Bill no longer worries that Peggy will be harmed when she is with her. Bill pays his wife alimony and child support for the period of time each day that she is with Peggy. His ex-wife constantly threatens to take Bill back to court to reverse the custody situation. Bill sees this as a ploy to get more money from him. Bill finds his ex-wife to be a great source of stress to him; yet he knows the value of her spending time with Peggy.

Jim, a father living with two children in Virginia, has had a totally different relationship with his ex-wife Alice. He and Alice started growing apart after seven years of marriage and thought they could no longer communicate with each other. The problems were probably made worse by Alice's job, which required her to work nights. This meant a shift in each of their roles. Alice had taken care of the children when they were babies; later that responsibility became Jim's. A trial separation, with Jim moving out and Alice balancing work and child rearing, ended in reconciliation. Jim resumed the responsibility for the child rearing. A few months later their marital problems began again, and this time Alice moved out of the house, leaving Jim with the children.

Alice moved out for a number of reasons. Primarily, she thought Jim had a better relationship with the children at this point than she did, and she believed his relationship with them would be damaged if he moved out. Secondarily, she was finding the forty-mile commute to her job in a large metropolitan area difficult. She and Jim also agreed that moving the children to the city with her would not be as beneficial to their development as letting them remain in a small community. Jim was happy to get the children.

Despite the forty miles separating them, Alice stays very involved with the children. She takes them to her home every other weekend. She attends school conferences, and Jim consults her about any major decisions that have to be made about the children. For Jim, Alice's continued participation in the children's lives makes parenting much easier.

The experiences of Allen, in chapter 1, afford another view of the type of visitation pattern and feelings that emerge between fathers and their ex-wives. Four years ago, Al's wife left him and their two children to pursue an affair with Al's best friend. Three months after she left, she returned. The new relationship had failed, and she wanted her children. But Al, who had struggled without her during that period, thought he was getting the hang of single parenting. He had seen other fathers doing it and believed he could, too. He had never given a thought to being a single father until his wife left: "I was not very involved with them before she left. The oldest was five. It was hard to get into little kids." A court battle followed. Even though the children were young, the judge was sympathetic to Al, and he won custody. It was decided that their mother could visit the children two weekends a month.

Needless to say, Al feels a great deal of anger and hurt toward his wife. The way the marriage ended and the way he perceived that she abandoned the children do not endear her to him. He and his ex-wife never speak. When the children are picked up every weekend, she knocks on the door, he opens it for the children, and they leave until Sunday. Al thinks she spoils the children terribly. He calls it the "candy man" syndrome. He says, "She dresses them up like dolls, gives them toys, and when the weekend is over, she puts them back on the shelf." There is no telephone contact between the two homes during the week; if one of the children is having a birthday, it is celebrated separately in each household. Sometimes, Al believes his children do not benefit from their visits with their mother and that both he and the children would be better off if she were not around. But at other times he admits that his children, especially his daughter, get something from seeing her.

The feelings expressed by Bill, Jim, and Al, and by other fathers, can often be connected to the reasons given for the divorce. The more the father blames the ex-wife for the divorce, the more anger and distrust exist. The fathers who cite their wives' infidelity as the reason for the divorce tend to feel the least positive toward them. Bill and Al believe their wives' behavior caused the breakup; they feel distrust, anger, and hurt. Jim, who feels the divorce was caused by their going their separate ways, does not blame Alice and still has warm feelings for her. Jim also feels sympathy toward her because he believes she was caught up in changing role expectations for women: "I feel sorry for her. She grew up hearing one thing about how women are supposed to act, and now she hears something else." Jim thinks people give her a hard time because she is not raising the children and, because he still cares about her, that hurts. Feelings of trust and caring exist between them even though the loving relationship they once had has changed.

## Feelings of the Ex-Wife

We have been hearing about the mother from the father's perspective. But regardless of how the father feels about his ex-wife and the type of relationship they maintain, the way the mother feels about her own situation plays an important part in maintaining a relationship with the children and the father. Noncustodial mothers feel discriminated against. This may mean that they avoid contact with the children and the father because they feel victimized. Some mothers may feel immobilized by guilt. Other mothers who have lost court battles, or do not have custody because their children picked the father, may feel too hurt to stay in contact with the children. The mother's financial situation, which is often shaky because of a lack of job experience, may make visitation between her and her children difficult if she lives out of state. About half the mothers in the study lived at least twenty miles away from the children. Phone calls in those instances become costly. The mother's financial situation may further inhibit visitation if she cannot afford to buy the children what she would like. Finally, if the father discourages contact because of his own anger at her, one more barrier to visitation is thrown in the way. Understanding these circumstances can help us change the negative stereotype of these mothers. Often they are the victims of circumstance.

The relationship that develops between the mother, the father, and the children is, then, affected not only by the initial circumstances under which the custody arrangement began, but also by the continuing relationship, the feelings of the family members, the aging of the children, the financial changes, and the comfort the mother may feel about her own situation. When the marriage has ended without a great deal of animosity, visitation may follow that is beneficial to everyone. Where unresolved feelings remain, and the anger that divorcing spouses hold toward each other affect how they parent and the amount of visitation, everyone suffers.

## Conclusions

A number of different points about the mother's involvement have emerged:

1.  Most fathers describe their ex-wives as being "somewhat" or "slightly" involved with the children.
2.  Almost half of the noncustodial mothers visit their children at least once every other week.
3.  The satisfaction the father feels with the ex-wife's involvement is based on the particular situation. There are fathers whose ex-wives are not involved and who are happy about this lack of involvement. Others wish their ex-wives were more involved. There are fathers whose ex-wives are very involved and who are happy with the involvement, and there are those who think the high level of involvement is troublesome.
4.  Generally, the more involved the ex-wife is with her children, the easier single parenthood is for the father.

One point needs to be reiterated. Aside from situations involving extreme circumstances, family members will benefit in the long run when there is regular contact among all of the members. It has been established elsewhere that single mothers and their children have an easier time adapting when there is regular contact with the father. Now, with a large sample of single fathers, we see that the fathers benefit from the noncustodial mothers' contact, too. Though this was not a focus of the study, the anecdotal information gathered suggests that children living with the father also benefit.

# 9
# The Father's Experiences with the Legal System and Child Support

One father, a mechanic, wrote: "I did not lose anything by going to court, because my ex-wife did not fight very hard. I am convinced if she had fought for the children [two boys, who were six and eight at the time of the breakup] I would not have been successful."

A management consultant, who was interviewed, told this story: "She left without the children. We decided I would have custody and she would visit. Then she decided she wanted to go to California, and she wanted the kids. She threatened, but never went for it. Then she attempted to snatch the youngest. I had had the foresight to get custody so I was able to prevent her from getting the kids, and the school was helping. She decided it wasn't worth it.

"We had some situations afterwards, which meant going back to court, but by that time I had established I could do a good job. But it required spending a lot of money, hiring a court psychiatrist. I had enough money, so I was fortunate. If you have enough, it can be easier. A lot of men I have spoken to have had problems. Basically, if you get your children at the beginning, you stand a good chance of getting them. Otherwise, all things being equal around here [suburban county of major eastern city], it goes to the woman. In situations where one person has a measurable problem, that makes it simpler. My ex had mental problems, which made it easier for her to not seek custody, and when she later sought it, it was too late. I had everyone behind me—the schools, family, even some of her relatives. I wanted the kids and was providing a healthy environment, so I got them.

"A lot of guys I have met seem to want their kids to get back at their ex-wives. That disturbs me. It isn't good for anyone. They want revenge. They are going for the vendetta. Some men sincerely do want to have their children and suffer because their children are not with them. . . . The men who want their kids to get back at their wife eventually probably do not end up with the kids. They decide it isn't worth it."

A third father said, "I feel that based on what I hear from other men, a man has to do more to prove himself than a woman does."

The custodial fathers' complaints are the most vehement, their tales of financial woe the worst, and their fears the greatest when they discuss their experiences with the legal system. They complain that they have to spend thousands to protect what is theirs; that mothers are given the upper hand; and that there is no guarantee that, once they have custody, a new judge will not reverse it. Their worries about losing custody are on-going. Nothing seems to upset their lives and frustrate them more than their court appearances. It is in this area that they believe they have the least control over their own destiny and are at the whim of an archaic set of values that, though no longer legally existing in most states, is still exercised by judges. As negative as are these fathers' feelings about their experiences, it must be remembered that these are fathers who won in court. Fathers who fight for and lose custody have even more complaints.

Fathers are seeking custody in greater numbers now than ever before. More equitable criteria are being used to determine if they are capable of single fatherhood. Some women claim the pendulum has shifted too far toward the father and the bias is now in his favor.[1] Some fathers, on the other hand, claim that the laws on the books, when they exist, often are not being followed. Many fathers seeking custody feel caught between progressive legal revisions that give equal weight to them in court and the values of the court personnel, which often hold that a mother should be raising the children. In the past, a father could get custody only if he proved his ex-wife unfit. Even then, before he got custody, he may have done battle with adoption and foster-care agencies that might have stepped in to make sure the child was being raised properly. The father's difficulty in getting custody led to a self-perpetuating cycle of assumptions that has been broken only recently.

As discussed previously, until recently fathers were perceived as being less important than mothers to the well-being of the child. Fathers correctly did not think they had a chance to get custody if they sought it. These two factors discouraged them from seeking custody and discouraged lawyers from recommending that they seek it. The cycle was completed when judges were discouraged from granting custody as they accepted all the assumptions. Winning custody of one's children became an impossible proposition for a father.

That has changed, and men now receive a fairer shake. In the 1970s such luminaries as Cary Grant, Marlon Brando, and Lee Salk won joint or sole custody of their children in widely reported disputes that encouraged others to seek custody. For many fathers, however, seeking custody is still an unnerving process in itself. The court system becomes the place where many angry feelings from the marriage are played out.

The legal system is many couples' only recourse for getting revenge. For example, when a partner's image has been damaged in the community by the spouse's extramarital affair, one way to get retribution is through the court system. Going to court gives these issues a public hearing. The hurt spouse can prove how bad the other person has been and can make that spouse pay for it—with property, money, or a loss of visitation rights or custody.

Although court is an excellent battleground in which to get back at a spouse, it is also proving to be a good place to resolve conflicts if partners are interested in doing so. A number of states and local jurisdictions are experimenting with or have instigated court-run mediation programs designed to assist spouses in property settlements and custody agreements. When these programs are available and the spouses are willing, a fair financial settlement can be made. Custody agreements can be set and visitation arranged with the help of court personnel who have more experience with these issues than the bewildered couple do.

Even with a warm relationship between separated couples, however, there can be difficulties in establishing such matters as a financial settlement.[2] A single mother from Detroit with custody of one son, who was interviewed for another study, provides an example. She and her husband parted on the best of terms four years ago. The decision to break up was mutual, as they both felt they were missing something in life. They made no attempt to legalize their separation until he became involved with somebody else. Until that point, he had taken care of his ex-wife financially. Suddenly it became clear to her that she had to look out for herself and assume an adversarial position toward her ex-husband. She had to make sure she received a suitable financial settlement. Whereas before he had always taken care of her, now she not only had to take care of herself but also had to fight him. All this was done as amicably as possible, but it changed their relationship.

When children are involved in the court proceedings, the stakes are higher because the welfare of the children is at issue. With drawn-out battles, a slew of professionals appointed by both sides and by the court may get involved. Expenses can run into the stratosphere as legal fees mount with each new court appearance. A 1977 *New York Times* article reported that a father seeking custody in a disputed case must be prepared to spend between $10,000 and $20,000 to win.[3] Today, costs can be much higher. The feelings that exist between the divorcing couple, whether as mother and father or as husband and wife, can make disputed custody battles horrible experiences for all concerned. Children are torn apart emotionally if they are forced to make impossible choices between parents. Judges are compelled to making Solomonic decrees. Joint-custody statutes, now on the books in over half the states, make some of these decisions easier. But when the mother and father do not live close by, or when they feel great anger toward each other, joint custody can become one more burden.

The responses given by the fathers in this study and the stories they recounted during the interviews show a wide range of legal and court-related experiences that may have more to do with the particular case, the lawyers involved, and the judge's reaction to it than to any legal precedent in force in a local jurisdiction, county, or state. Many fathers found judges and court personnel biased toward the ex-wives; other men found judges very sympathetic to their situation. This variability fuels the growing debate between proponents of both the women's and the men's movement, both of whom claim to be the underdogs.

Only a few of the studies on single fathers with custody discuss the legal problems the men have faced. Gersick (1979) made this issue a focus of his study. Over half of the forty custodial and noncustodial fathers he interviewed felt great dissatisfaction with the legal system and with their lawyers. A number of fathers stated their lawyers had been incompetent; others thought their lawyers had been overly sympathetic to the wife. Naturally, the fathers who did not have custody had more complaints. A number of the noncustodial fathers had decided to not press for custody because of their lawyer's recommendation that it would be hard to achieve. Gersick concludes that there is great variability in these men's experiences, which is further complicated by class issues. Professional men feel better about their lawyers than do nonprofessionals. It must be noted that Gersick completed his research in 1976. Nearly ten years later, at the time of this writing, it can be anticipated that much has changed.

## Fathers in This Study

As discussed in chapter 3, almost 20 percent of the fathers in this study won custody of their children following a court battle. From interviews, it was obvious that these fathers felt much more strongly about court-related issues than did the fathers who used the courts to rubber-stamp what the mother and father had agreed to privately.

The father's experience with the legal process is based, in part, on his contact with lawyers and his appearance in court. Some positive and negative aspects of contacts with lawyers and court personnel were found, depending on the father.

## Lawyers

The part the lawyer can play in the father's experience is vital to the success of the custody situation. Slightly less than half the fathers in this study responded on the questionnaire that they sought the advice of a lawyer for getting custody. Of those who saw lawyers, 21 percent found them very helpful, 38 percent found them somewhat helpful, and 41 percent found their lawyers not at all helpful.

Arthur Yellin, who was interviewed for ABC's "20/20" program in the late 1970s, drew national attention because of his attempt to win custody from his wife of his then six-year-old son. In an interview, he described an expensive and long legal battle that affords insight into the importance a lawyer can play in helping a client get custody. According to Mr. Yellin, his lawyer, Philip Solomon, had two basic strategies with this particular custody battle. No attempt was ever made on Solomon's part to prove Arthur's ex-wife unfit. Instead, the attempt was made to prove Arthur to be the more competent parent. This was achieved by Solomon's getting Arthur to present himself as a stable person and as a stable father. He was discouraged from making comments to the effect of, "I will be destroyed if I do not get my son." It was Solomon's feeling that these remarks could be interpreted negatively by a judge and influence the judge's view of Arthur's competence. Arthur's strategy was effective.

From the lawyer's perspective, single fathers can be difficult to represent. The lawyer has to ascertain whether the father has a chance to win custody. If the lawyer accepts the case, she or he has to decide which issues to raise in court and how much to involve the children. The lawyer is well aware that their inclusion may cause those children great stress. He or she has to provide some feeling about the judge who is trying the case if that information is known, and may have to offer moral support to the father and counsel him on how to present himself. The lawyer has to negotiate child support, visitation, custody agreements, and property settlements. Finally, the lawyer needs to pay special attention to the nature of the bias toward or the prejudice that may exist against the mother. These factors can make working with the father as a client a risky business. Of course, these factors translate into problems for the father, too. Some of the fathers' stories show what working with a lawyer under these circumstances can be like.

John works in a refinery and is raising two children. His wife walked out on him and then wanted to get custody. His salary is around $27,000, and he reports feeling strapped financially by his legal fees. When asked about his experiences in court, he replied: "Lousy. The lawyers, too. I finally did find a lawyer after the first one did nothing. He was not for anyone but he knew I was getting the shaft. My wife, believe it or not, was getting $30 a week and I had the kids. My first lawyer had said to me no way I would have to pay alimony. But he was wrong. I did, and then I lucked out. She was living with her boyfriend and she let the children know about it. What she was doing with the alimony was going partners with him. She was working and they were splitting all of the bills. I notified my new lawyer. 'Don't send more alimony,' he said. Her lawyer found out about it and we went to court. In fact, I went to court four times. I saw the judge, though, only once. Everything was always settled outside the courtroom.

"One time we got there and when my lawyer saw who the judge was, he told me I was going to get screwed. He said we were going to have to work out a deal before we got in there. We talked her lawyer into something real fast!"

Like John, Skip had some positive and some negative experiences with lawyers. His first lawyer helped him get custody but then stopped practicing family law. When Skip's wife later sued for custody, he got a new lawyer who did not think fathers should raise their children. "I switched from him real fast. I then got a woman lawyer. She was O.K., and I still have the kids."

Jack, another father who was raising three young children, had a more positive experience. "My lawyer was good. He was friends with the judge. The judge seemed to lean over backwards to me when I came before him. He chewed out my ex and gave her visitation but me custody. She did not have to pay anything. For me, the system worked fine."

A fourth father, Marvin, raising three teen-agers, had an easy time, too. "No problem [with the court system]. My lawyer told me what to expect. But I did not get any [financial] support, and sometimes she gives a little money but it is nothing you can count on."

## Fathers Who Used Lawyers

There were certain characteristics related to the father who sought legal assistance. These fathers tended to be younger, to be raising younger children, and to have had custody for fewer years than those fathers who did not see lawyers. Those fathers who sought legal help naturally are also more apt to have gained custody through a court fight. These findings may indicate an interesting trend. The fact that older fathers and fathers who have had custody for longer periods of time have not sought legal help, and have been able to get custody on their own, indicates that the way the fathers achieved custody in the mid-1970s was different from the way they achieve custody nowadays. Younger fathers are using lawyers; this may mean that a different breed of father is fighting now—one who believes he has a chance to win in court.

## In Court

As the father goes through the necessary stages to gain custody of his children, if the case is disputed he winds up in court. When he gets there, it is often impossible to predict what will happen. Idiosyncratic judges enforcing fuzzy laws make much of what happens in courts a crap shoot. This point was illustrated by two cases cited in chapter 1 in which courts reached opposite conclusions concerning mothers' abilities to parent.

Fathers in this study reported meeting judges who were convinced that children must be raised by their mother. It is only under extraordinary conditions that these men have won. Not only do they believe they have to go further than a mother to prove their competence, but they often are strapped with large alimony payments, and their ex-wives are exonerated from paying child support. These experiences upset and anger many of the fathers.

One father, Dick, thought he had no protection from the courts, even though he originally gained custody. One year later, when he was making plans to remarry, he had to go back to court because his ex-wife was again petitioning for custody. "We went through a five-month ordeal and went to the court psychiatrists. We went to court while I was making wedding plans. The day of the hearing, she withdrew because the child wanted to be with me."

Another father, Jeff, who eventually won custody of two children, lost his first battle. "I wanted custody from the start. I filed for divorce and custody. She lied in court and I got the divorce, but she got custody. Women can get men arrested here [a southern state] at the drop of a hat. She cost me my job and $30,000. She had them [the children] and said she was going to move with them to Texas. I got a restraining order to keep the kids and her in the state so they stayed. She stayed with them for a year and a half, and then I got documentation that she was immoral and got them back under a change of custody.

"The courts are heavily biased. They made me feel ashamed to ask for custody. Laws seem equitable but are not practiced by the older judges, as they should be. They stereotype a lot. To get custody, you have to be head and shoulders above your wife. Fathers don't seem to get custody when the wife is seen as competent."

A third father, Michael, found bias on the part of the court personnel even though he won custody. "There was initial arbitration for custody. My wife had deserted us and was not really sure if she wanted the children. I took advantage of her psychological disorders and won custody. But the arbitrator kept asking my wife to reconsider giving up custody."

These fathers, like many others who were interviewed, believed they were at a disadvantage because of their sex. They thought they had to work harder to get custody than their wives would have if the situation was reversed. They also felt their wives were relieved of financial responsibility because they were women.

One father said, "My wife was very far in arrears. If it was me in arrears, I'd be in jail."

## Child-Support Issue

The court must also rule on the difficult question of child-support payments. The issue of the noncustodial parent paying support has drawn a great deal of attention in the last few years. The focus is invariably on the father being held responsible for paying when the mother has custody. This is not surprising. The Census Bureau recently noted that fewer than half of the women awarded child-support payments are collecting the full amount.[4] The focus is also on the father because there are many more of them and they are usually the primary breadwinner in the family. Many mothers with custody have horror stories equal to those of the fathers!

Child-support payments have come under increased scrutiny during the last few years for a number of reasons:

1. When the noncustodial parent does not pay the child support he is supposed to, the onus often falls on the state and federal government to support the family financially. The government has become increasingly willing to enact stricter laws to force the errant parent to pay. One approach used is to attach wages.

2. Child support has come under scrutiny as a feminist issue. Although feminist philosophy on the one hand advocates women taking care of themselves and not relying on men for financial and emotional support, it also recognizes the needs of women and their right to get what they deserve. Many mothers who are not working or have few job skills are seen as being rightfully in need of support. The mother's role in the intact family is seen as being as important to the maintenance of the family as the father's, so it is believed she should continue to receive compensation after the family breaks up.

3. Similarly, there is a feeling afoot that both parents should share in raising a child. If both parents should share equally in the raising of the children during the marriage, there is, as Cassety (1984) points out, a "moral" obligation for that to continue after the breakup.

Along with this increased focus on child support has come a concomitant interest in why fathers (usually the noncustodial parent) do not pay support. A number of reasons have been given:

1. Many fathers claim that recent harsh economic conditions and high unemployment have made payments difficult to make.

2. Fathers often believe the judge has been biased toward the mother and has set an unreasonably high amount to be paid. This feeling runs especially strong when the ex-wife is working outside the home and earning a decent salary.

3. The intermingling of the issues of child support and visitation. Fathers frequently claim they are not paying child support because their visitation rights have been withheld or that visitation is made difficult to arrange. At the same time—and it is a chicken-and-egg argument—mothers claim they make visitation difficult because the father has not met his financial obligations. Often, a standoff occurs in which the father says he will begin paying when he can see his children more easily, and the wife in turn offers greater access to the children when he starts to pay. Sometimes the father does not pay because he does not approve of the way the mother is spending the money on the children.

When the father has custody, a different set of considerations applies to a discussion of child support. These considerations were highlighted by the fathers during interviews. What emerged were essentially two distinct categories of fathers: those who do not want support, and those who do. Fathers in each of the categories gave a number of reasons for their stance on support.

### Fathers Who Do Not Want Support

In this category, four reasons were frequently mentioned:

1. Many men do not encourage the mother to pay support. Because of societal norms, some fathers think it is an insult to their masculinity if the mother pays support. Especially if the father has been the sole support of the family, having his ex-wife pay him support for the children he is raising makes him uncomfortable. The circumstances surrounding the breakup may affect this feeling. The more anger the father feels toward his ex-wife based on the nature of their marital split, the more the father may expect the wife to pay.

2. Some fathers believe it is too much trouble to have the wife pay. They are unsure if the wife is trying to buy something by her payments. If she does pay, they fear she will have more influence over the children.

3. Some fathers do not want support payments because they think that if they come to rely on the money and it stops, it will make their life more complicated. Being self-sufficient is easier for some of the fathers than having to rely on their ex-wives' largesse.

4. Finally, there are fathers who fear that having the ex-wife pay support will improve her standing in the eyes of the court. If she decides to contest the custody arrangement, she will be able to show proof of her continued interest and involvement in the children's well-being.

### Fathers Who Want Support

Three reasons emerged frequently with fathers in this category:

1. Some fathers reported feeling that because they were now carrying the whole load of the children, their ex-wives naturally should pay support, just as they would if the ex-wives had custody. They see it as a fairness issue.

2. Other fathers are motivated by the notion that it is important for the children to have the mother paying at least a token amount. This keeps the mother involved with the children and gives the children the feeling that their mother still cares about them, as she is still paying something toward their support.

3. Some fathers need the money to maintain an adequate life-style.

If the father does want payment, getting it can be a sticky matter. The judges seem reluctant, especially in cases of disputed custody, to give the children to the husband *and* ask the mother to pay child support. Giving the children to the father is difficult for many judges; asking the mother to also pay support is, in the eyes of some judges, pouring salt in her wounds.

There is also the purely economic issue. Many mothers did not work during the marriage; once they left the marriage, they started earning wages that were much lower than the fathers'. Expecting them to pay when they are either on welfare, receiving alimony, or working at a low wage seems unreasonable to many judges.

These issues and the different desires of the fathers make the payment of child support a complex problem that strikes at the core of the fairness question. Is it fair for a noncustodial mother to be required to pay at least something if a noncustodial father also must pay something? Should these issues be decided purely on economic grounds? Or should they be decided with an eye toward greater sharing of child-rearing responsibilities, regardless of economic factors? Should the fact that women in the United States earn less than men[5] be sufficient cause not to expect women to pay child support? Finally, of course, the mother's desires must be considered. There is no easy answer, although these questions must be considered when the fathers' experiences in these areas are discussed.[6]

Although there was no specific survey question that asked whether the mother was paying child support to the father, this issue was explored in follow-up interviews. The answers provide some background for what was just discussed.

An estimate based on those follow-up interviews is that between 10 and 20 percent of the mothers were paying some child support to the custodial father. An enormous range of financial arrangements was found. Many fathers were clearly ambivalent and expressed feelings similar to those of one father who said: "I feel discriminated against because of not getting child support. But a man is reluctant to force his wife to pay when he feels she is just getting by." This anger was often accompanied by the awareness that the ex-wife did not have much to give. Most of the fathers with split custody (the father and mother each had a child) were paying their ex-wife alimony and child support. One example involves a father who earned over $60,000 and was paying $1,250 a month to his wife, who was raising two of their three children. Another father who had custody a majority of the time was paying his ex-wife child support for the time each week that the child visited her. With the families in which the mother did pay, it was often a minimal amount. More common were informal arrangements in which the mother would buy clothing or toys for the children. Although this type of gift-giving was not formalized, it did reduce the financial burden on the father.

Three fathers who do receive some support payments are examples of the way this issue has been handled. Ed is a private investigator from West Virginia. His ex-wife has remarried, lives in a nearby state, and visits the children every so often. On the issue of child-support payments, John says: "I did not get any support payments when I got custody through the courts [three years ago]. But sometimes now she gives a little money, but it is nothing you can count on. She is helping out with college a little bit. Payments come from her in how the mood strikes her. She works off and on. In a year she may give $500 for the whole year, though last year she gave $2,000 for college for my oldest."

Bill, an electrical engineer earning over $40,000, also has been receiving occasional payments for the two children he is raising. "She paid no support to me until she regained custody of our youngest. She has remarried and does not work. Her husband is making some of the payments for her. I liked it better when I carried all of the freight, and now that she is paying part, there are more problems."

Joe earns $20,000 a year; his ex-wife, a real estate broker, earns about the same. She pays him child support of $200 a month for the two children he is raising. He said she has never been late with the money.

Most fathers do not get payments. Those who do receive them have gotten them both through court settlements and informal agreements. Usually, the more contact there is between the father and the mother, the more apt the mother is to be paying something. Of course, the more money the wife earns, the more she is likely to be paying. As one father suggests, however, the amount of income one earns should not be an issue for a noncustodial father or mother. He thought it very important that his wife pay at least something every month, even though she has no job and is on welfare. He believes even having her pay $1 keeps her involved with the children and gives her the feeling she is part of their caretaking. That can be helpful to her, the father, and the children.

## What the Fathers Need

Despite, or perhaps because of, their treatment at the hands of lawyers and the court system, over 60 percent of the fathers reported that receiving more legal support was the area that would be the most helpful to their adjustment. Although slightly over half of the fathers reported that they had sought legal help, only slightly more than half of those who saw lawyers found their services helpful. Clearly these fathers have a great many concerns about the legal system. Again, these are the feelings of fathers who do have custody.

## Conclusions

The status of the father as he travels through the legal system has changed dramatically over the last decade. Even though there is great improvement, many fathers still believe they are discriminated against when they seek custody. This feeling of discrimination has been shown to discourage some men from even attempting to seek custody, and makes those fathers who do seek it more wary. In talking to fathers and from looking at the history of custody disputes, it appears that fathers are increasingly getting a fairer shake in court. The more often men seek custody, the more people in the legal system will view them as competent single parents. Whether the pendulum will swing too far toward the father—a sign of a backlash against women and mothers—is yet to be seen. The recognition by everyone that both mothers and fathers need to have adequate access to the child is the beginning point in sorting out the difficulties.

# 10
# Mothers with Custody/Fathers with Custody

T his chapter will provide a broad framework against which the findings from the study of fathers with custody can begin to be compared. Although the thrust of this book has been to describe what happens when fathers have their children alone, it is also important to go one step further and consider how these fathers with custody compare with single mothers with custody. This step will permit a fuller understanding of the single-parenting phenomenon, the experiences of single parents, how they feel about their situations, and what their differences are. In addition, research on mothers without custody has also been undertaken; this research will provide further information on the single-parenting phenomenon.

One important caveat must be included. Comparisons between the data discussed here have to be done with caution because of the way the data were gathered. As discussed, the data for the fathers' study were gained from a questionnaire placed in *The Single Parent* magazine, the magazine for members of Parents Without Partners. The questionnaire was placed prominently in the magazine. The fathers merely had to pull it out of the magazine, complete it, and mail it in the stamped self-addressed mailer that the questionnaire formed. In addition, local PWP chapters had been encouraging member fathers to complete the study for a month before it came out.

The data from the mothers with custody were gathered by placing a small advertisement in the same magazine. Mothers with custody were asked to send a self-addressed stamped envelope to me for a copy of the questionnaire the fathers had used. Some words had been changed to reflect the sex of the respondent. The mothers were then directed to fill it out and return it to me. This required a mother to: (1) see the small ad; (2) address a letter and include a self-addressed envelope; (3) complete the questionnaire when it was received; and (4) mail it back to me. The mothers who made up the final sample for this comparison study were mothers who read the magazine closely enough to see the ad and were motivated to follow through on the steps necessary to complete the questionnaire process. Hence these mothers may differ in unknown ways from the fathers who filled out the questionnaire with much less effort. A sample size of 150 mothers with custody of children eighteen and under was obtained. This is a very small proportion of the approximately 100,000 mothers with children eighteen and under who belong to PWP, who were estimated to have qualified for the study. These mothers, then, may not be representative of PWP members who are mothers with custody.

Finally, this ad was placed one month after an article discussing the fathers' study was published in the magazine. As they indicated in letters requesting the questionnaire, reading the article influenced some of the mothers to write to take part in the study. It is difficult to determine what effect their having read an article about custodial fathers had on their motivation for requesting a questionnaire and on their answers.

Despite these significant limitations, there can be value in these comparisons. Both groups consist of single parents who are members of a self-help group and were interested enough to fill out the questionnaire. The mothers' responses add an important counterpoint to what we know about fathers. The comparisons, then, should be viewed as representing possible but not definitive trends in the similarities and differences, particularly between middle-class single parents with custody.

Before discussing the comparisons in depth, it can be briefly summarized that although there are differences between the fathers and mothers in the amount of satisfaction and comfort they encounter in the parenting areas examined, they experience the greatest amount of difficulty in the same areas. In other words, the easiest and most satisfying areas for both groups of parents are housekeeping and establishing a relationship with the children; the hardest are working while rearing children and adjusting to being single.

## Background of the Mothers

The mothers' average age was thirty-eight years old, slightly younger than the average age of the fathers in the study. The average length of custody, at 4.7 years, was a little over a year longer than the fathers', indicating that the mothers have had slightly longer to adjust to their situation. More of the mothers (19 percent) described their marital situation as separated than did the fathers (14 percent). The others gave their marital status as divorced.

The mothers came from thirty-four different states and Canada, as compared with the fathers, who represented forty-eight states and Canada. Their average income, at $15,642, was significantly less than the $28,325 averaged by the fathers. In some cases this figure included alimony and child support; in others it did not. This is also the case with the information given by the fathers about their income, although the likelihood of their receiving alimony or child support is much less. This gap in income indicates the potential for significant differences in the life-styles of these parent groups. The amount of education completed and the racial composition of the groups were similar.

Half the children being raised by the mothers were male and half were female. (The fathers were more likely to be raising boys than girls by a three-to-two margin.) The average age of the children, at eleven years old, is similar to the average age of the children being raised by the fathers. Differences did appear, however, in the percentages of young children—9.5 percent of the children being raised by the mothers were four years old and younger, compared with 5.8 percent of the children being raised by the fathers. There were 262 children eighteen and under being raised by the 150 mothers. The average number of children being raised by the mothers was similar to the number being raised by the fathers (1.7). Of the mothers, 45 percent were raising one child, 32 percent two children, 17 percent three children, and 6 percent either four or five children. Only three mothers had children eighteen or under living elsewhere, a much smaller percentage than for the fathers.

The fact that there were some differences in the sex and age of the children being raised by the mothers and the fathers may be due to tradition. Usually, following a divorce, the mother gets custody. No differences in the sex of the children she is raising would be expected. For the father to get custody, however, there may have been a court battle that ended with the judge deciding the father should be raising a son. In addition, the slightly greater number of younger children being raised by mothers than by fathers may reflect the prejudice both parents and courts hold against fathers raising younger children alone.

## The Situation Surrounding the Divorce

Just as the fathers had indicated that they were less likely to have initiated the breakup, these mothers gave the complementary response. They were more apt to say that they had initiated the breakup, that they wanted the marriage to end, and that they were not surprised when it did end.

The reasons given for the divorce also showed some differences between the groups. In considering the figures about to be presented, it must be remembered that a respondent could give more than one reason for the divorce. The reasons given most often for the divorce, by 29 percent of the fathers, were shared reasons—ones that indicated both he and his wife were responsible. This reason was given by more mothers (40 percent). The spouse's infidelity, mentioned by 25 percent of the fathers, was given by 38 percent of the mothers. The ex-wife leaving—a reason indicating that she wanted to end the marriage—was given by 24 percent of the fathers. As is consistent with responses discussed, this reason is much less common among those given by the mothers, as mothers tend to end the marriage more often than fathers do. Only 15 percent said their marriage ended because of their husband's leaving. The fourth most frequent reason, given by 16 percent of the fathers, was that their spouses had problems that caused the marriage to end. This was given third most frequently by the mothers, mentioned by 22 percent of them.

It is interesting to note that 12 percent of the mothers said the marriage ended because of the husband's immaturity and lack of responsibility, a response given by only 3 percent of the fathers. Six percent of the mothers responded that physical abuse ended the marriage, as compared with only three fathers (less than 0.3 percent). Because mothers tended to give more reasons for the divorce per questionnaire than fathers, comparisons are difficult.

## The Reasons for Custody

Almost by definition, the circumstances surrounding the way a single father gets custody are apt to be out of the ordinary. Because mothers with custody are obviously more common, the ways they get custody are more familiar. Comparing these two groups sheds light on the extent to which the fathers' ways of obtaining custody are out of the ordinary.

To the question, "Did you want sole custody?" the mothers were much more apt to respond affirmatively: 83 percent of the mothers said they wanted it very much, compared with 66 percent of the fathers. Only one mother said she did not want custody at all (0.7 percent), as compared with 6 percent of the fathers. The other responses were as follows: 3 percent of the mothers wanted custody "somewhat" as compared with 10 percent of the fathers, and 13 percent of the mothers wanted joint custody, as compared with 17 percent of the fathers.

These answers show a greater reluctance on the part of these fathers than on the part of these mothers to assume custody. At the beginning of their custody situation, these mothers are less likely than the fathers to be reluctant warriors in parenting. This is an important point, because the desire to have custody is linked with the satisfaction fathers feel with their parenting.

The greater reluctance on the part of the father to have custody and the fact that it is a nontraditional arrangement for him contribute to making his situation initially harder than that of the mother. This is proven by the answers to a question about the level of stress surrounding the decision to have the children stay with the custodial parent. The mothers indicated that there was little stress experienced by everyone involved when they got the children. Fathers reported much greater stress for both them and the mothers.

The reasons the mothers gave for getting custody also showed marked differences from the fathers' responses. For example, it is more likely for these fathers to get custody through a court battle than for these mothers. If fathers seek custody, it is often because they believe they have a chance to get it. At the same time, the mothers were more likely to list mutual agreement as a way of gaining custody. When the marriage broke up, it was more likely for the mother to have custody and for the father to agree willingly that she should have it. When the father gets custody—an unusual circumstance—his impression of how he got it may reflect reasons that were more easily specified among the choices offered, rather than grouped under broad headings. Greater justification is needed for the father having custody than for the mother having custody because the former is more unusual. Hence general reasons such as mutual agreement are less likely to be given.

Two other responses merit discussion. Only 13 percent of the mothers gained custody because the children picked them, half the percentage of the fathers who gained custody that way. With the mother getting custody, such issues as the children choosing the parent may not come up. Both parents may agree that the father having custody is not an option. Before the father got custody, his being the sole custodian may have been offered as an option to the children. For the children living with their fathers, there is a greater likelihood of this being one of the reasons.

The case of a parent getting custody because the other could not handle the children also merits discussion. Although only one mother (0.7 percent) said she had custody because her husband could not handle the children, 20 percent of the fathers gave that response. This most likely means that the noncustodial father's competence is not an issue when the mother gets custody. This is largely because many parents think that mothers should have custody. Therefore, even if the father was seen as being incompetent or unable to handle the children, that incompetence would probably not affect the decision for the mother to have custody. It is, however, very much of an issue when fathers get custody. In fact, in many instances, their wives' incompetence compelled them to seek custody. The following table shows the responses (respondents could give more than one answer):

*How Was It Decided You Would Have Custody?*

|  | Mothers | Fathers |
| --- | --- | --- |
| I won custody suit | 13% | 20% |
| Mutual agreement | 50% | 37% |
| Children picked me | 13% | 26% |
| He/she wanted a career | 3% | 8% |
| We agreed I was better parent | 13% | 14% |
| Wife/husband remarried | 5% | 3% |
| Ex could not handle children | 0.7% | 20% |
| I abducted the children | 0.7% | 2% |
| Ex did not want a court fight | 4% | 11% |
| I offered a more secure home | 27% | 22% |
| Ex was too ill | 3% | 5% |
| Ex deserted the family | 15% | 20% |
| Children needed female/male model | 2% | 2.6% |

## Parenting Issues

Chapters 4 through 8 of this book deal with five major parenting areas that single fathers face raising children alone: (1) housework and child care, (2) work, (3) the relationship with the children, (4) socializing, and (5) the relationship with the ex-wife. The mothers' responses will be compared with those of the fathers in these areas to provide an impression of where differences between these groups of parents exist.

### Housekeeping and Child Care

In chapter 4 the housekeeping activities of the fathers are examined in terms of who did the housekeeping during the marriage, who does the housekeeping now, and how comfortable the fathers are with the housekeeping chores.

Mothers who gained custody, as would be expected by tradition, described themselves as being much more involved in the housekeeping chores during the marriage than their husbands. In only 1 percent to 2 percent of the marriages did the fathers have primary responsibility for any of the housekeeping chores. Of the fathers who gained custody, approximately 10 percent said they had primary responsibility for the cooking, cleaning, and laundry; and 21 percent said they had primary responsibility for the shopping. Assuming some exaggeration by respondents who may tend to overemphasize their own role, these figures indicate that in most of the marriages discussed in this book, whether the mother or the father ended up with custody, the housekeeping was the mother's job. A comparison of responses also shows that fathers who gain custody were slightly more involved in housework during the marriage than fathers who do not.

When asked about the current responsibility for the housework, both groups of single parents gave similar answers. In each group, the parent was likely to hold primary responsibility for cooking, laundry, and shopping; with cleaning, the responsibility was more likely to be shared by the parent and the children. In all categories of housekeeping, a higher percentage of mothers were apt to have the primary responsibility than of fathers. The fathers were more apt to share the chores with their children or to give the children the responsibility for the chore. In addition, the fathers, usually by a differential of three to one, were more apt to use outside help.

The finding that mothers do a greater percentage of the housework when they have custody than fathers do is unsurprising, as it would be a continuation of the pattern established during the marriage. Also, the children being raised by the mother are somewhat younger than those being raised by the father and are, therefore, less capable. For the fathers, many of whom had to familiarize themselves with the housework, sharing it with the children even to a slight extent did not require a change in an old pattern but, rather, a way to handle new tasks. The same factors that govern the father maintaining many of the chores himself also hold for the mother.

As might be expected, as single parents, the mothers reported greater comfort than the fathers in all housekeeping activities. Cleaning, for both groups of single parents, was the task they felt the least comfortable doing.

## Child-Care Arrangements

The mothers, like the fathers, do not find arranging child care overly difficult. The fathers, perhaps because of their higher income, reported a slightly greater degree of satisfaction with the child-care arrangements made. The mothers were more likely to be mixed in their satisfaction on this issue.

The specific child-care arrangements made by the parents for their children after school were compared. One-fifth (21.6 percent) of the fathers who were raising children in the five- to eleven-year-old range left them alone after school. Almost precisely the same percentage of mothers raising children in the five- to eleven-year-old range (20.6 percent) left these children alone after school. The percent of latchkey children for these groups of parents are similar, although their situations are different for three reasons:

1. Fathers earn more money and can afford child care more easily than mothers.
2. A greater percentage of mothers than fathers are not in the work force at all or are in the work force part time, enabling more of them to be home.
3. Fathers who work may have more job flexibility because of higher job status than mothers who work.

Compared with the other areas of parenting that confront single parents, the areas of housekeeping and child care are handled with relative comfort and satisfaction. The issues are ones that both groups of parents are able to handle. Mothers report greater comfort with housekeeping, and fathers report slightly more satisfaction with the child-care arrangements made.

## The Single Mother and Work

Fathers found balancing the demands of work and child rearing one of the two most difficult areas. Only one-fifth said this was not at all difficult, and most others reported numerous job changes because of demands of parenting.

Mothers with custody reported much more difficulty. Only 10 percent said that work had not been difficult; 23 percent of the mothers, as compared with 14 percent of the fathers, said it had been "very difficult." (It must be noted that although 90 percent of the women listed some occupation, no question asked whether they were currently employed. Hence there is no way of knowing how an unemployed mother who is supported by her ex-husband would have answered the question concerning the difficulty balancing the demands of work and child rearing. Also, a few of the fathers were unemployed.)

There were some similarities and differences concerning specific job-related changes experienced by mothers and fathers. These comparisons have a good deal to do with the nature of the work being done by fathers as compared with mothers.

Some of these changes—reducing travel and reducing work load—are most likely attributable to the nature and the amount of work done by men versus women. It is interesting to see that nearly twice the percentage of mothers as fathers had to quit or were fired from their jobs. These differences might be even more extreme when we consider that many mothers may not have been working. Also interesting is the similarity in the amount of work missed, the need to work flexible hours, and the time missed because of child rearing.

*What Job Changes Have You Experienced Due to Being a Single Parent?*

|  | Mothers | Fathers |
| --- | --- | --- |
| Bringing work home | 18% | 11% |
| Reducing travel | 9% | 32% |
| Reducing work load | 9% | 19% |
| Working flexible hours | 22% | 23% |
| Having to miss work | 32% | 34% |
| Arriving late or leaving early | 32% | 35% |
| Being fired | 7% | 4% |
| Quitting | 12% | 6% |

Raising children while working causes more difficulty for the mothers than fathers. Three possible explanations can be given for this:

1. They may be less satisfied with the child-care arrangements they made during their workdays.
2. They may have limited job flexibility, associated with their lower income.
3. If they did not work outside the home during their marriage, their entry or reentry into the work force may be difficult.

## Being Single

Establishing a social life and adjusting to being single again were more difficult for both mothers and fathers than were the adjustments of parenting.

Comparing the two groups of single parents points up some differences. As would be expected, the single mothers dated less often than the single fathers; 56 percent of the mothers dated at least every other week, as compared with 73 percent of the fathers, and 11 percent said they never dated as compared with 6 percent of the fathers. Not only do mothers date less, but a comparison shows they are slightly less satisfied with their social lives.

Even though the mothers have less active and slightly less satisfying social lives, there are indications that they may feel slightly more comfortable being single again; 55 percent said they felt comfortable in that area, as compared with 47 percent of the fathers. The fathers may find more difficulty being single again because they are less likely to have chosen that status than the mothers. Perhaps for a similar reason, the fathers have a slightly harder time dealing with loneliness; 62 percent found dealing with it difficult, as compared with 55 percent of the mothers. It also may be harder for fathers to adjust to being single because the role of custodial father is less institutionalized than that of the single mother. Because there are more single mothers to provide examples of how to handle parenting issues, socializing, work, and so on, mothers may have an easier adjustment process.

The fathers' dating activity may improve their social lives, but it does not have a carryover effect into the way they generally feel about being a single parent. Mothers feel more secure about being single when they are wearing the single-parent hat. Regardless of these differences, adjusting to a divorce when you are raising children full time remains a task that is hard for many single parents to master.

### Relationship with the Children

The other area that presents the most satisfaction for the custodial parents is the relationship they have with their children. The amount of satisfaction experienced by the mothers and fathers with respect to the relationship with their children and with how their children were doing (over 75 percent were satisfied with both) was almost identical. In addition, the ratings they gave themselves as parents were very similar.

The mothers were more involved with their children in disciplining and in doing activities during the marriage than were the fathers who had custody. Only between 1 percent and 4 percent of the custodial mothers described themselves as taking a back seat to their husbands in these areas during the marriage, compared with between 7 and 12 percent of the fathers who described themselves as having done less than their spouses.

Two things are clear from these responses. From both the mother's and the father's perspective, fathers are more involved in disciplining and doing activities with the children in the intact family than they are in housekeeping. For the families represented here, based on the responses, fathers who ended up with custody were more involved during their marriages in disciplining the children and participating in activities with them than were fathers who did not end up with custody. The same was true for housework.

Although one important conclusion that emerged from the chapter on the father's relationship with his children was that he felt more comfortable raising younger children than older children, no such result was found for the mothers. No differences were found among the mothers in the satisfaction they felt in their relationship with either older or younger children. One reason could be that these mothers were better prepared for the demands of parenting children of all ages, knew what to expect, and were able to adapt to each developmental stage more easily. Although the overall satisfaction for both groups was the same, the individual differences between fathers raising older and younger children (as discussed in chapter 6) may have been due to a lack of knowledge about what to expect with older children and to the father's need for more control.

### Relationship between the Noncustodial Parent and the Children

The last areas to be compared deal with the feelings and the amount of contact beween the custodial parent, the noncustodial parent, and the children. One point to be explored here has to do with the stereotype that the noncustodial mother stays more involved with the children after the divorce than the noncustodial father. The first question deals with the qualitative amount of involvement, the second with the quantitative.

To the question "How involved is your ex-spouse with the children?" responses by the mothers with custody and the fathers with custody were identical in two of the visitation categories and differed in two others. With both groups of parents, 7 percent of the ex-spouses were described as being "very involved," and between 23 and 24 percent of the ex-spouses were "somewhat involved." In two other categories of responses, however, the noncustodial mother was depicted as having greater involvement. In the mothers' study, 43 percent of the women described the noncustodial father as being "slightly" involved, and 27 percent described him as being "not at all" involved. In contrast, 49 percent of the custodial fathers described the noncustodial mother as slightly involved and 20 percent described her as not at all involved. From the comparisons, the noncustodial mother is slightly more likely to be involved with her children than the noncustodial father. Differences exist here yet they are not extreme.

Marked differences appeared though in the satisfaction the custodial mothers and fathers experienced with their ex-spouses. Only 27 percent of the mothers said they were satisfied with the noncustodial father's involvement with the children; whereas 65 percent said they wished he was more involved; and 7 percent thought he was too involved. Fathers with custody expressed much more satisfaction: Forty-seven percent of them were satisfied with the noncustodial mother's involvement; 44 percent wished she would be more involved; and 9 percent thought she was too involved.

Two probable reasons emerge for the differences in these responses. First, the fathers report more involvement from the mothers, which could lead to greater satisfaction. Second, and conversely, the fathers may respond to the negative societal sanctions against noncustodial mothers. The fathers, like many other people, may look down on these mothers because they do not have custody. They may be more satisfied when there is not much involvement from the noncustodial mother. In other words, many fathers do not have the mother's involvement and are happy with that situation. At the same time, the mother with custody may have a tendency to be dissatisfied with the father's involvement because she may equate involvement with child-support payments. A lack of payment by the father—something that is perceived differently from a lack of payment by the noncustodial mother—is likely to taint the mother's satisfaction with the father's involvement. These parents may be responding more to the idea of the involvement and the differential expectations placed on men and women than to the actual involvement. In fact, the frequency of involvement is remarkably similar.

## Frequency of Involvement

With the exception of a percentage of fathers who were described as never seeing their children, the visitation patterns described by the mothers and fathers with custody were virtually the same. For the mothers, 21 percent said there was visitation at least once a week from the noncustodial father, as compared with 24 percent of the custodial fathers reporting that frequency of visitation from the noncustodial mother. On a biweekly basis, visitation was reported by 23 percent of the mothers and 22 percent of the fathers, and 14 percent of both the mothers and fathers said visitation occurred on a monthly basis. Fifteen percent of the mothers said visitation never occurred, as compared with 9 percent of the fathers. Responses for categories of visitation on holidays, during the summers, and in the category labeled "infrequently" were similar.

The relative similarity in frequency of visitation in the groups may be unique to these samples. Furstenburg and colleagues (1983), comparing the visitation patterns of noncustodial mothers and fathers from a variety of socioeconomic classes, found more marked differences between mothers and fathers, with noncustodial mothers visiting significantly more, than were found here. Other comparisons between their study and this are difficult because the categories set up to examine visitation were not the same.

Greater differences were found in the number of overnight visits spent with the noncustodial parent. Noncustodial mothers were described as spending more overnights with their children than noncustodial fathers. The custodial mothers said their children spent an average of 1.3 overnights with the father, as compared with 1.9 nights per month being spent with the noncustodial mother. In addition, although almost half the fathers said their children never spent any overnights with the mother, nearly 60 percent of the mothers described that pattern between their children and the fathers.

In general, although the visitation patterns for the majority of the noncustodial mothers and noncustodial fathers are similar, there is a likelihood that a greater percentage of noncustodial fathers than noncustodial mothers will have no regular contact with the children.

## Conclusions

A number of conclusions can be drawn about these two groups of parents with custody. It can be broadly stated that fathers with custody experience difficulties and satisfaction in the same parental areas as mothers. Differences do appear between the groups in the extent of the difficulties experienced, in how they ended the marriage, and in how they gained custody.

The mothers were more likely to have ended the marriage than the fathers. They were also more apt to blame the failure of the marriage on infidelity, to feel the reasons for the ending were shared, and to indicate that the husband had problems. Fathers are more likely to say the marriage ended because the wife left. Custody was more likely to be gained by the father following a court decision, because his ex-wife could not handle the children, and because the children chose him as their parent. Mothers are more likely to get custody because of a mutual agreement. Fathers are less apt to say they wanted sole custody than mothers.

Housework and arranging child care are not difficult for either group of parents. More problems were experienced by the single parents in attempts to balance the demands of work while raising children. In this area, the mothers had a more difficult time than the fathers. Socializing also was difficult for both groups of parents, with comparisons between the groups showing mixed results. Fathers dated more and were more satisfied with their social lives, but mothers felt more comfortable being single again. Establishing a satisfying relationship with the children was equally satisfying for both groups. The results concerning the amount of contact between noncustodial parents and the children were generally similar, with a somewhat greater likelihood of noncustodial fathers having no contact with the children than noncustodial mothers.

One can interpret these comparisons between custodial mothers and fathers in a number of ways. For instance, we could say that tradition or societal conditioning are the reason both for the similarities and differences between groups. Mothers have traditionally fulfilled many of the same roles in the intact marriage that they continue to fulfill after the breakup. Their experience in the home serves them well, and their lack of experience and status in the workplace hurts them. The fathers, moving into unfamiliar areas, do experience some problems compared with the mothers. But the problems the fathers encounter in areas in which they have almost no experience are not much greater than those the mothers encounter in the areas in which the mothers do have experience. Tradition hurts the fathers because they cannot find many role models to follow or many single fathers as friends with whom to identify. This adds to their feeling more uncomfortable in the role of single parent than mothers, who may have acquaintances who are also single mothers.

We could also say that money is the big reason for the differences between mothers and fathers. Mothers may socialize less in part because of their lack of discretionary income with which to hire sitters or to entertain themselves the way they would prefer. Lack of money also reduces their options for child care during the day. Their financial situation could be linked to tradition, also. Women have less experience in the workplace, hence fewer entrees into the workplace, and therefore less income.

Since mothers and fathers have difficulties in the same areas of parenting, we can conclude that it is not the sex of the parent that makes the difference when it comes to being a single parent; it is the task that has to be accomplished that matters. Single parents have problems in the same areas because those areas, particularly working and socializing, are the most difficult. The difficulties cut across different upbringings that men and women have had, the role conflicts of fathers and mothers, and the lack of role models. Housekeeping is simply not that difficult for anyone; adjusting to a divorce and establishing a single life again certainly are.

It should be emphasized here that the purpose of this discussion is not to conclude that either mothers or fathers have an easier time overall with single parenting or are better at it, but rather to tease out the roots of some of the similarities and differences that exist. What we can say is that as mothers and fathers were both raised in our society and are currently part of it, they are affected by many factors in their parenting. One goal of this discussion is increasing the strengths single parents have and reducing their problems. The findings are sufficiently similar, when it comes to the difficulties a parent has with adjusting, for us to conclude that there are common problems that all parents face. The tasks that have to be accomplished make single parenthood, for the most part, a unisex status. Men and women have to deal with the same issues. Their success or failure with these issues depends to a large extent on the issue, and to a lesser extent on conditioning and financial means.

# 11
# Children of Single Fathers

*Geoffrey L. Greif*
*Kathryn L. Wasserman*

In 1983 the number of children being raised by single fathers had risen to nearly 1 million.[1] There is every indication that this number, which has increased dramatically over the previous decade, will continue to increase as long as there is a high divorce rate and more opportunities exist for men and women to share all of the responsibilities of home life.

It is important for us to learn about these children. Their experiences being raised by a father tell us a great deal about how children of divorce cope in general and, specifically, the success of this increasingly common postdivorce family. Their own words and reactions tell us more about what happens between children and their mothers when the mother is the visiting parent.

This chapter makes no attempt to draw sweeping conclusions about the children. Other research has studied the children in depth.[2] Instead, the intention is to draw attention to some of the issues that children being raised by their fathers may face and to look at the single-father-headed household from the children's perspective. The children's own words tell a great deal about the wealth of experiences they have living with their father.

Twenty-one children, ranging in age from two to nineteen, and members of eight different families, were interviewed by the authors. Five of the eight fathers belonged to PWP and had taken part in the survey. The other three fathers were found through lawyers working with the families. All but one of the interviews were conducted in the families' homes. The interviews lasted between one and two hours; in some cases, where there were younger children, two interviews were conducted. Occasionally, role playing and picture drawing were done with younger children. The father was present during most of the interviews and was also interviewed separately for background information. Of the twenty-one children, twelve were female.

With the exception of two fathers, one lawyer and one scientist, the fathers were blue-collar workers. Their incomes were below the $28,000 average of the fathers in the survey and much closer to the national average for all single fathers. The fathers' professions were mechanic, carpenter, painter, electrician, welder, and switch operator. One of the fathers had been unemployed for six months at the time of the interview.

Both a male and a female interviewer were used to give the children more opportunities for interaction. It was believed that having a female taking part in the interviewing would be of particular interest to girls being raised by the father, who might form a different relationship with her than with a male interviewer. This did prove to be the case with one of the girls.

## Tug-of-War

In many families where there has been a divorce, the children get involved in a tug-of-war between parents who do not agree about who should raise them. The divorced parents seek custody of the children for a variety of reasons, ranging from a genuine desire to raise them, to revenge, to financial gain. In these situations the children may be tossed back and forth between warring parents, each trying to look out for the best interests of the children while also trying to achieve what best meets their own needs. The children are acutely aware of what is going on and are often troubled by being placed in the position of having to choose between parents. Just because the children are living with their father—the less common arrangement—it does not mean they are immune from their parents' wrangling. As is obvious from the children interviewed, when the father has custody the pain felt by the child can still be great.

Sally is twelve and the oldest of four children. As the oldest, she feels the tug-of-war between her parents more than her siblings do because she is rapidly approaching the age at which she will be the first to be asked by the judge whom she wants to live with. Her father has been raising the children for the past six years, ever since the children's mother left him for his business partner. Initially the mother did not want the children. Over the last two years, however, she has begun to take the father into court to try and regain custody. Sally's father thinks their mother wants custody to avoid paying him child support.

Sally is feeling the pressure. She says: "I have to decide because I can't keep on thinking about it. If I go with my mom, my dad will be angry and my grandfather won't like it. I don't know what I am going to do. They are always fighting over me. I am in the middle because they have to decide things about me and that is when they start to fight." Sally believes she will lose her father's and grandfather's affection if she lives with her mother. She also does not want to be separated from her brothers and sister. Yet, with an awareness of the future and a questioning of how comfortable she will feel in a father-headed home, she said: "I am starting to develop. I wear a bra sometimes [her mother bought it] and I don't know what else will happen. I need my privacy sometimes, and Mom would be better about that."

In another family, the father is struggling to hold on to his three children largely for financial reasons. His two youngest want to return to live with their mother, who has filed for custody of them off and on over the last few months. The father is currently receiving $12 a week in support payments. If he loses custody of his two youngest children, he will have to pay $100 a week in payment to their mother, a sum that would greatly impinge on the life-style he would have with his oldest child. There is also another reason he says he wants custody—one that has nothing to do with money. His ex-wife is living openly with a female lover, and he does not feel that is a good atmosphere in which to bring up children.

## When the Children Decide

Although a tug-of-war is not uncommon, in many situations the father and mother, when they separate, let the children decide whom they want to live with. When the father has custody, this can often be a Hobson's choice: It appears to be a choice, but there is only one real option. For many of the children interviewed, one choice was to stay in their own home with their father, maintain their friendships in the neighborhood, and stay at their school. The other was to move with their mother, who is often unemployed or earning much less money, to much worse surroundings and a strange neighborhood.

In one family with two girls and two boys, the children were offered this type of choice. The oldest in the family is Tracy, who is now nineteen. She describes how she saw their options: "We could have gone with our mother, but the place she was going wasn't very nice. She was going on welfare and the place had rats. She did not know if she was going to have a job or not. Here, we knew we could stay with our friends and have better stuff."

In another family the two daughters were given a choice of whom they wanted to live with, and then one of the choices was withdrawn. Joan and Jill were eighteen and sixteen when their parents separated last year. The children were asked to choose whether they wanted to stay in the house with their father or move into an apartment with their mother. Joan wanted to stay with her father: "I grew up here. This is where all my memories are. I have my own room. If I want to say, 'Leave me alone,' I can go up to my room and shut my door. At my mother's, I wouldn't be able to do that. I couldn't have my own room. And my privacy is the thing that really kept me going."

Jill, after much agonizing, decided she wanted to stay with her mother, who was pleased to have her. Before Jill could move in with her, however, her mother became involved in a new relationship that prohibited the move. So Jill, although it is not her preference, is living with her sister and father.

## The Toll Taken

Just as it is not easy for children to be separated from their father when the mother has custody, so it is not easy for many of the children interviewed to be away from their mother. In many families the mother was the primary caretaker and homemaker during the marriage. When she moves out, a great number of adjustments have to be made.

Although Tracy and her siblings decided to live with their father largely on the basis of the conditions of the two homes and the security of their father's job, it is a decision that has taken its toll. Adam, the youngest, misses his mother a great deal, even though he sees her almost every week. He said he likes living with his father because he can be alone in the house. What does he do when he is alone? He calls his mother to talk to her.

The children in this family also feel their mother has replaced them in her life. She has remarried, and they feel awkward and resentful when they visit her. When asked about the marriage Tracy said: "I guess I felt a little funny because she always used to say, 'I am never going to get married again,' but she went out and did it." This takes its toll, too.

Aside from the hurt the children feel over not seeing their mother, the reaction of others often has to be dealt with. Living with one's father is still a rare phenomenon, and these children may have been ostracized for it by their school acquaintances. Yet only one child said: "The kids at school make fun of me. They say, 'Why aren't you with your mom? What's wrong?'" None of the other children reported any problems in this area.

This is not to say that the children, even those who do not receive outside reminders of their living situation, are not keenly aware of what is going on in their homes. In the play of one seven-year-old girl whose parents are fighting over her, there were frequent references to a lawyer calling on the telephone. There were also signs of the tenuous position this child feels she occupies in her household. When playing with dolls she set up a scene where she said: "Who is going to have the babies? They can be such a pain."

Sometimes the strain that children of divorce go through is not easily verbalized by them, especially when the children are younger. Instead, the strain comes out in the needs they show. One ten-year-old girl formed a very quick attachment with the female author, taking her to her room and showing her new clothes and a stuffed animal that was still unnamed. This girl gave the impression of needing an older female friend. There can often be a need to try out behaviors or make contact with an adult of the opposite sex of the parent who is raising the child.

An additional toll is taken when children are being used as pawns in their parents' battles. The children interviewed who had been involved in such battles were more cautious than children whose parents were amicably working out their differences. Having lived in an atmosphere of custody battles and heated arguments, these children have adapted by scrupulously avoiding taking sides or giving information that may increase the tenor of the battles. Those children who were not fought over seemed freer to talk.

## Living with the Fathers

For a variety of reasons, the children's experiences are different when they begin living with their father than when they were living with both parents. For sons, it may mean getting away with less; for daughters it may mean getting away with more in some ways while also taking on new, more adult responsibilities. For all the children, being raised by a father has meant doing more housework than they did when their mother was still home. The extra work was a common complaint among the children interviewed, and it was usually acknowledged that the house did not look as neat as it had before. The meals may taste different, too. As one boy reported, "Dad's a good cook, for a man."

Adam and his older brother, though enjoying the freedom they have because neither of their parents is in the home as much as they used to be, feel they have to watch their step more around the house now. Their father has always been strict, but their mother used to intercede on their behalf when he came down too hard on them. Now they watch less television and are being held more accountable for their whereabouts when they are not home. The strictness has its benefits, though. Adam's schoolwork has improved a great deal since his mother left.

Tracy and her sister have a different reaction to living with their father. Tracy feels she can manipulate him better than she could her mother. "I can tell dad I need a new hair spray and he'll go out and get it for me. When mom was here she would say: 'No way you're getting that expensive stuff. You can make do with this cheaper can.' It's stuff like that. I can fool him more."

Sally and Tracy are both the oldest children in their families and assume the most responsibility. For Sally, this means doing the cooking when her father is out and taking charge of the cleaning. Tracy also does the most cooking in her family. The other chores are shifted between the children on a regular basis that is judged to be fair by everybody.

The extra responsibility Tracy carries is not limited to cooking. She provides emotional support to both parents, as she did even when they were married. She takes it in stride. "When things were going bad with Mom and Dad, my mother used to talk to me about it. Now that she's gone, Dad sometimes stays up until 3 A.M. talking with me. I'm listening to him but I am also falling asleep."

Joan and Jill reported sharing the housework with their father, a situation that sometimes causes problems. Joan said: "It's a big change with the work load. Mom used to do most of it. Now, everyone has to do their share, and there are times when people can't or don't do their share and there are big fights then. But overall I would say we have had a pretty good deal here, all things considering."

Despite the extra work, Joan feels it is easier living with her father: "Mom would want more than my father would. She always has, and she worked for a clean house. Now we are more equal in the house."

It is not always the oldest child who gets saddled with the most responsibility in the absence of the mother; sometimes it can be the oldest daughter. She may be the one the father naturally turns to for help and the one who most willingly takes on the extra work. In one family where there were two boys, sixteen and twelve years old, and a fourteen-year-old daughter, it was the daughter who was doing the most housework. Her father described her as being the most reliable and as doing things without being asked. It was sensed that she did not object to this arrangement and saw it as her way of contributing.

Most of the children seem to feel that the expectations for them to finish their housework were greater but that the quality when it was finished was lower. In other words, their father was stricter about them completing their chores but did not set as high a standard as their mother might have. As mentioned elsewhere, many fathers who are raising children alone adapt to the demands by letting the overall quality of the housework fall to a level below that of the home during the marriage.

## Sticking Together

The children in these families seemed to pull together after their parents' breakup. The absence of the mother, which usually came following months or years of fighting between their parents, may have made the children afraid of fighting. Having seen their parents fight and then break up, the children may try to avoid it. The mother's absence may also remove one of the sparks that kindled the fights.

Joan and Jill fight less often now than they used to, for two reasons. First, they do not have the time to fight because of the extra work load they are assuming. Second, their mother used to intervene in their fights, which worked more to escalate than to end them. Their father does not intervene, so the fights end sooner.

Reducing the fighting is a form of mutual protection that helps some of the children deal with the uncertainty of their living arrangements. Most children see fighting as one more sign of danger and a warning signal that their family may split further apart. As might be expected, however, in one of the families interviewed, the fighting increased with the divorce. The chaos of the home and the stress from the divorce pitted the children against each other rather than pulling them together.

Sometimes, when anger does flare (as is normal and healthy for all families), the children may lash out at their father. He becomes the target because he is available and because the tenuousness of the children's relationship with their mother makes an attack on her riskier. There is the fear that the mother, if she is the brunt of their anger, may reduce her contact. As a result, the children may become defensive concerning the mother in an unconscious endeavor to hold on to the relationship with her or to win her back. They become protective of her in an attempt to counteract their own feelings of anger toward her and to make the home a nicer place for her to return to.

## What is Unique about Children of Single Fathers?

All children whose parents are divorced have to go through a number of transitions, which can range from the beneficial to the detrimental depending on their home life before and after the divorce. It may be, however, that children being raised by single fathers have a different experience than those raised by single mothers. No attempt is being made here to draw broad generalizations that apply to all children being raised by single fathers; the number of children interviewed is too small. Nevertheless, some tentative conclusions can be reached about the experiences of these twenty-one children based on contact with them.

One difference may be in the amount of housework the children do. A father who has to assume a number of home-related duties his ex-wife most likely did during the marriage will be more apt to share those duties than will a mother who was handling them all along. Having to do housework was a common complaint among the older children, who did a great deal less when their mother was present.

Second, in the cases where the children interviewed still had regular contact with their mother, there was a great deal of interest in her well-being and in spending time with her. There was also a sense of protectiveness that the children exhibited toward their mother. Whether they felt the need to defend their mother because she was a female, because she was often living in worse circumstances, or because they usually had known her better than the father is hard to know. Since interviews were not conducted with children living with single mothers, a comparison of the amount of interest displayed by children living with the fathers could not be made to see whether the same feelings would have been shown for the father by children being raised by their mother. If, as is true in most cases, the mother was more involved with the children before the breakup than was the father, it would seem that separation from her would be more difficult for the children than separation from the father *only* insofar as it is a change from the known to the unknown. This could be mitigated by the nature of the relationship that has developed in the past and continues to develop between the parents and the children; it is not a statement that mothers should be raising children instead of fathers. It might very well be that even though these children expressed great interest in the mother, they would have fared a lot worse if they were living with her.

Third, the experiences of the daughters are clearly different from those of the sons. The daughters interviewed here were assisting in housekeeping more than the sons, even when there was an older son in the family. This may mean that a daughter is being overburdened while a son is not doing his fair share. Such a message from fathers could be detrimental to both daughters and sons.

In addition, daughters' experiences are different because of issues concerning female sexuality. This area is a concern to some of the daughters living with their father. A father and son most likely feel more comfortable confronting this issue.

Again, this is not to say that daughters are any harder to raise than sons or that they should not be raised by fathers. Like many developmental concerns, female sexuality can be handled in a number of appropriate ways, as suggested by the fathers of these children. Some fathers bought books to help them discuss sexuality; others, who felt less comfortable or sensed their daughters' discomfort, asked friends, relatives, or teachers to provide education.

The age of the children is also important to consider. For Joan and Jill, who had already passed through puberty when they began living with their father, this was not a problem. Joan also feels that if she and Jill were living with their mother, having all females in the home would make it less of a "family situation." With a man in the house, she feels more comfortable because her home more closely corresponds to her idea of a family.

Fourth, we were struck by the quick attachment formed with us by the younger children we interviewed and the difficulty they had in separating when it was time for us to leave. Sometimes the children would follow us to our car. Other times they would invite us back for another visit. These younger children's needs for adult attention seemed marked, especially in contrast to the wariness exhibited by many of the older children interviewed.

Certainly, many of these conclusions lend themselves to more rigorous future investigations. Wallerstein and Kelly (1980), for example, have already embarked on a longitudinal study of children being raised in a single-parent family. One look into the future of children being raised by a father was provided by the family interviewed in chapter 2.

As mentioned, all children must go through a number of transitions when their parents divorce. The children interviewed here, for the most part, and despite some rather traumatic experiences, were resilient. They possessed a spark that, when fanned, showed that they were survivors, that their life went on regardless of which parent was with them a majority of the time. Yes, their experiences living with their father are different than what they would have been living with their mother. But those differences provide an opportunity for growth—a challenge most seemed willing to confront happily.

# 12
# Conclusions

S end me the results [of the survey] quickly. How many other freaks are there out there like me?" This was the response of one distressed father to the questionnaire.

The purpose of this book has been to examine the myths about single fathers with custody and provide a better understanding of fathers and of single parents in general. To this end, the preceding chapters have attempted to show what these fathers experience as they face the different tasks of parenting. Although most fathers claim to be satisfied with the majority of their parenting tasks, wide variation exists. This book has shown some of the characteristics of those fathers who are doing well and of those who are having problems.

The fathers reported that they tend to feel comfortable with the housework and child-care arrangements they have made. They also tend to be satisfied with their relationship with their children and with how their children are progressing. They have more difficulty in balancing the demands of work while child rearing and in adjusting to being single. Dealing with the legal system also proved troublesome for many fathers. The fathers were mixed in their satisfaction with their relationship with their ex-wives. Overall, their adjustment is similar to that of the single mother.

Which fathers generally seem to have an easier time being a single parent? A few characteristics emerged that are often present in fathers who were adapting well:

1. They have higher incomes or report that they feel comfortable financially.
2. They were involved in housework and child rearing during the marriage.
3. They have attributed the marital breakup to shared reasons; they do not place blame entirely on themselves or on their wives.
4. They are satisfied with their child-care arrangements.
5. They have ex-wives who are involved with the children on a regular and frequent basis. Some of the fathers in this group, however, were having a particularly hard time because of the ex-wife's involvement.
6. They sought custody or said they wanted sole custody at the time of the breakup.

Some of these characteristics not only helped the father when he got custody, but led to his getting it in the first place. For example, the fact that he was involved in housework and child rearing during the marriage may have helped him believe he could raise his children and also let the mother know that he was competent to raise them. These characteristics, along with some suggestions provided by the fathers, form the basis of strategies that fathers can use to help themselves, or that others can use to help single fathers in their adjustment.

## Strategies

Perhaps foremost among the strategies is resolving the relationship with the children's mother. When relations between the parents are smooth and there is regular and nonacrimonious contact, everyone seems to prosper. In such a situation, two parents are working together as a team and help each other out in raising the children. The children are not caught in a web of marital discord. The parents can separate their feelings for each as divorced spouses from their responsibilities as parents. Obviously, as was shown in many of the situations described here, that is not always possible. It is recommended, though, that single fathers make every attempt to keep the mother involved with the children.

Second, good child-care arrangements went a long way toward easing the father's transition. The time it took to find someone to take care of the younger children when the father was not home was time well spent. When there is good child care the fathers and the children feel more comfortable.

Third, many fathers discussed the benefits of setting up a routine or schedule at home so everyone knew what his or her responsibilities were. This proved to be an effective way of managing the home and of assuring a sense of family cohesion. Having a schedule provides a method for family members to know what is supposed to be done and where everyone is.

Fourth, a strategy concerning the father's relationship with his children emerged from a write-in question on the survey. This centered on the importance of being involved in the children's lives and also of drawing a line between being a parent and being a friend. For many fathers, taking part in PTA meetings and school conferences, as well as spending time alone with the children, was new. The fathers found they enjoyed becoming more involved in their children's lives, and many encouraged such involvement. Some fathers warned of the danger of getting too involved in their children's lives, trying to become a friend, and losing their effectiveness as a parent. Single fathers then need to be wary of confusing too many roles. The responsibilities of being a parent come first.

Fifth, the fathers found meeting other single parents helpful. Because they were members of a self-help group, this would be expected. They found such involvement beneficial both for the support they personally received and for the activities in which their children participated. These activities gave the

the children a chance to meet other children of single parents. Socializing with other single-parent families is recommended as one step in the adjustment process.

Sixth, and finally, the fathers appreciated being accepted and understood as single parents. They benefited greatly from people who took the time to get to know them and who did not attempt to stereotype them. This gave them permission to be themselves. To that end, the fathers found that talking about their situations and their feelings helped them. Discussions within the family also helped the children face the realities of living with a father rather than a mother. To help the children face these realities, community programs and services designed to educate all members of the community about single parents are recommended, as are programs designed to facilitate communication within all families.

It must be stated that fathers in this study could also have adapted well without these characteristics and without following most of these strategies. Many fathers have a great sense of self-esteem that they either had before they gained custody or achieved afterwards. This feeling of self-esteem can be the key to how fathers adapt. In fact, the level of self-esteem of the fathers interviewed seemed generally high. This could be attributed to a number of factors. Being the custodial parent may give the fathers a sense of accomplishment and a sense of belonging. Many fathers took pride in what they were doing. It also may be that men with high self-esteem are more apt to seek custody and, because they feel good about themselves, their wives may feel more comfortable relinquishing custody.

## Drawing Broad Conclusions

The task at hand now is to draw broader conclusions that will help our understanding of other parents—single and married, male and female—and of children, and to put these findings into perspective. With these conclusions, I have emphasized the importance of the findings and applied them to our knowledge of sex roles. These conclusions are first presented briefly and will then be discussed in depth.

1. The dichotomous view that society holds of single fathers comes from a lack of understanding of them and is detrimental to all single parents. This dichotomous view perpetuates myths and protects our stereotypes.
2. To a large extent, it is not the sex of the parent that makes parenting difficult or easy, but the task with which the parent is confronted.
3. It is impossible to weigh whether single fathers as a group or single mothers as a group have an easier time adapting to single parenthood.

4. The importance of learning about single fathers' experiences is that more men will be willing to seek custody and more women will be willing to relinquish it.
5. Such knowledge also will encourage both mothers and fathers to consider joint or shared custody.
6. Exploding the myths will help both children of divorce and children in the intact family.
7. Men's roles have shifted somewhat over the past decade. We are not moving quickly toward an androgynous society. Many men are changing in reaction to the changes women are making. Fathers with custody have been pushed to change the most.

The conclusions to be discussed here are based both on the findings and my own impressions of men's and women's roles. These are impressions that are optimistic about the future and somewhat pessimistic about some of the claims made about the present.

1. *The dichotomous view that society holds of single fathers comes from a lack of understanding of single parents. This dichotomous view perpetuates myths and protects our values.*

People's reactions to the single father and their treatment of him are dichotomous. On the one hand, single fathers with custody of their children are viewed as being extraordinary individuals. They are praised by friends and strangers alike for their stability, their caring attitude, and their dedication. For further proof of this special treatment afforded single fathers, ask most single mothers with custody. They will readily point out the lack of support and, in some cases, the ostracism they experience because they are single mothers.

The special treatment afforded the father has another side to it, however. These fathers are perceived as needing help and, in some cases, as being incompetent. They are seen as unable to handle housework and child care on their own. Well-intentioned friends and relatives rush to their aid much sooner than they would to a single mother's. School officials want to meet with their ex-wives rather than with them. People assume the fathers use an enormous amount of outside help to deal with the housework. If they cannot afford such help, it is assumed that they rely on their parents or on a live-in lover. Few people believe they can handle the housework and the children on their own. This is the double bind that exists for the father. Praise and admiration for being a sole custodian are coupled with questions about his competence.

Why do single fathers receive this double whammy, and what are its implications? The answers to these questions are interrelated. Single fathers are treated this way because of tradition. For almost everyone now alive who lived with both parents, the mother raised the children while the father supported the family financially. As a result of this history, when a father has custody, people believe something unusual must have happened and rush to his aid. Seeing the father fulfilling the role of single parent goes against the grain in a number of ways. Fathers receive these reactions because people are not used to seeing men in this role. When knowledge is lacking, people fall back on their values to form a reaction. They rely on their stereotype of what men should be like and react to them without real knowledge. What is protected is the stereotype held by the viewer; it is the fathers, children, and mothers who get hurt.

Single parents receive this treatment not only because of tradition but because of the current state of fatherhood. Most fathers are not as involved with their children as are mothers. It is rare to see fathers in a park with children during normal workday hours. The results of this dichotomous treatment of fathers are many, and they have wide-ranging implications for parents.

## The Single Father with Custody

For the single father, this special treatment can be upsetting and confusing. Many fathers do not believe they are extraordinary people. They feel they are simply doing their job by taking over the children. They are unnerved by the attention; it puts them on guard. In dating situations they wonder whether woman are seeking them out because of who they are as people or because they are good father material. Some men are offended by the offers of help, which they see as a putdown of their own abilities. Not all men resent the help, of course. Some appreciate help and seek it out to reduce their own workload. Nevertheless, help is offered because it is assumed the men will need it, when in fact most of these fathers eventually feel comfortable handling household chores. It is in the workplace, in the emotional adjustment to being single, and in the court system that they feel they need help. In those areas, not much help is forthcoming. Because of this dichotomous view, fathers feel misunderstood and do not get the kind of help they do need.

## The Married Father and the Noncustodial Father

The father who is married and the noncustodial single father are also greatly affected by this view of the single father with custody. It is a view that these fathers may share, and it may scare them away from seeking custody if the situation presents itself. If they accept the myth that fathers with custody are extraordinary, and if they do not feel extraordinary themselves, they may not seek custody. Married fathers also may shun opportunities to take part in child rearing. These two groups of fathers may be scared away by what they perceive as their own lack of ability, when in fact they may have as much ability as the typical father with custody had before he began raising his children.

Conversely, if fathers accept the myth of single fathers' incompetence, they may not want to put themselves in that position. Fathers who are contemplating seeking custody may believe it is better to be viewed as normal and competent in a noncustodial role than as incompetent in a custodial one.

## The Single Mother with and without Custody

For single mothers, the impact is different. The mother with custody wonders what all the fuss over the single father is about. She certainly gets none of it. She is not seen as extraordinary, and she is not offered help. For the noncustodial mother, the special attention given the father is salt in her wounds— a reflection of how bad she must be for not having the children. Their roles are seen as complementary. If the father is so wonderful, it must be because she has been so terrible. For noncustodial mothers this is far from the truth. Many mothers give up custody for the well-being of the children. Instead of being praised, they become the lightening rod for negative misperceptions.

Members of both groups of mothers see the attention afforded the fathers as one more example of the deferential treatment afforded men. Women have seen such deferential treatment in the workplace for years, and it galls them to see it happen with parenting as well. The praise the fathers receive and the lack of appreciation afforded mothers degrade them and minimize both how many of these women spend their time and the way they define themselves. Some married mothers feel this, too.

Very few people gain anything from the myths that surround single fathers or from people's reactions that grow out of these myths. Most single parents do not feel understood and accepted for what they are; rather, they feel stereotyped for what they never were.

2. *To a large extent, it is not the sex of the parent that makes parenting difficult or easy, but the task with which the parent is confronted.*

The fathers and mothers who were studied have the most difficulties in the same areas: working while child rearing and adjusting to being single. Three main reasons, which overlap, can be given for why working and adjusting to being single are difficult for both groups of parents: (1) the lack of role clarity; (2) tradition; and (3) the similar stages through which families pass.

## Lack of Role Clarity

Sarbin and Allen (1968) have written that a person's behavior will be less predictable and less satisfying when there is a lack of clarity of role expectation. A lack of clarity, they write, occurs in three different situations: (1) when there is vagueness about what is expected; (2) when there is a ". . . lack of agreement among occupants of complementary roles"; and (3) when there is ". . . incongruity between the role performer's own expectations for his role and the role expectations held by those comprising his audience" (pp. 503–505).[1]

For the single father and single mother, taking care of housework and establishing a satisfying relationship with the children do not cause a lack of role clarity. The housework and the laundry do not talk back to them—although in some families, as in the one described in depth in the second chapter, disagreements between parents and children can get played out in that area. With the children, the role of the parent is also clear. According to Sarbin and Allen, there would be no vagueness about the parent-child role. The roles of parent and child are complementary, and usually the parent and child agree on the parent's role (to a normal extent, excluding debates about car keys, dating, and homework).

There is a lack of role clarity in many other areas. When the single parent has to work and raise children, problems arise. The issues facing the single father and single mother in the workplace are not the same, however. The father usually entered the work force believing he would be able to pursue a career. The responsibility for the children is expected to fall to the mother. When the father is no longer able to pursue job progression at work with his old vigor because he is raising the children, he has to change his view of himself. For many men, abandoning long-held career goals is hard. His boss also may be unhappy with his parenting status. She may have hired him with the expectation that he could work late, travel, or change his shift at her request. When the father begins to balk at such requests because of parenting responsibilities, the boss may begin to look elsewhere to get the job done, bypassing the father.

The single mother's circumstances are different. She is less likely than the father to have been hired with expectations that she would be as dedicated to the job. This is an unfortunate reality of being a woman in the workplace. It is harder for her to achieve the job status and security that a man has achieved. Hence the pressure on her from the boss if she has to come in late or leave early will be different than that felt by the father. At the same time, the expectations for achievement mothers hold for themselves when it comes to working are often lower than those held by most fathers. Many women have not been raised from birth to believe they are going to compete in the work force. Men have. Their psychological adjustment to the role of worker *and* that of parent is not the same. However, mothers' adjustments are at least if not more difficult. For example, mothers often lack some of the perquisites of an influential position, which come with more years on the job or may come if one is a man. These so-called perks include being able to set up a flexible schedule. Also making it difficult for many mothers is a lack of clarity in their own mind concerning their commitment to work while child rearing. Often financial demands force them to work. Yet work and single parenting do not mix.

A lack of role clarity also exists for the single parent who is trying to adjust to being single again. The father or mother has to deal with a number of issues for which the expectations are not clearly defined. These issues make socializing a natural repository of problems. Dating after a divorce, whether one is a parent or not, is often difficult because it means confronting one's sexuality with a new partner and accepting the end of the marriage. Many divorced people are unsure of how to act when they begin socializing. When there are parental responsibilities, problems mount. It is tough to be a social being with sexual needs while also staying up late to help a child make a Winnie-the-Pooh costume. In addition, socializing is seen by many parents both as taking time away from the children and as confronting them with the possibility of a replacement parent. If the parent feels guilt in the first place for the breakup of the family, socializing can become one more activity to avoid in order not to hurt the children further. Finally, socializing and adjusting to being single force the parent to deal with acceptance or rejection by others. Single mothers often experience more rejection than acceptance. Single fathers, by contrast, often feel too readily accepted. In either situation, the reactions of others may not be based on the individual characteristics of the parents, and this is unfair.

Socializing raises a host of issues for the single parent. Once these issues have been confronted and socializing begins, the single parent may not be sure how to act or how to meet the expectations held by others. Regardless of the parent's sex, this lack of congruity in roles results in stress.

There is a second reason that single fathers and mothers have difficulties in the same areas: *tradition.* There are no successful role models for managing parenting and dating or parenting and working. Successful role models do exist for managing parenting and housekeeping, two functions that have been associated with each other for a long time as the major domain of the mother when she has sufficient financial support. No one has yet been able to institutionalize the combination of the other areas. Involvement in one has made involvement in the other difficult. A great deal of tradition and conditioning have to be bucked when both are combined. Regardless of whether it is the mother crossing over into the traditionally male realm of work or the father crossing over into the traditionally female realm of parenting, problems arise.

Third, *the stages of development through which these families pass are similar.* All families have to adjust to the same naturally occurring changes. Children start school, which changes the family situation. They grow up and leave home, necessitating another family change. In between are minor markers that also affect the family. Children become teenagers, go to work part-time, start dating. These natural events signal changes for the whole family. Each event is a mini-crisis for the family members as their function in the family changes. Single-parent families are, of course, not immune to these changes; in fact, they may be more susceptible to them. With only one adult present, the options for adapting are more restricted. Minor crises arise in the family when the custodial parent starts dating, as this means a change in how the children and the parent view each other. It is the structure of these families with one adult in the home that results in these events taking a similar toll regardless of the sex of the parent.

What we have, then, are families evolving over a period of time who are trying to cope with normal developments, their single-parent status, and the new roles that come with these changes. These changes are universal and have to be faced whether one is a single father or a single mother.

## Implications

The similarity between the mothers and fathers regarding their parenting experiences has important implications for who raises the children. If it is the role of the single parent and the tasks involved, not the sex of the parent, that makes single parenting difficult, then sex as a criterion for deciding who is the most fit parent should be discarded once and for all. Yet the tender-years doctrine is still being used.

A change in this assumption is supported by the finding that the degree of comfort the fathers feel with housework and children is not significantly different from that experienced by the mothers. Mothers should not be given the advantage over fathers in disputed custody cases because of an assumption that, as women, they will be able to handle these particular areas more easily than men.

Fathers should not count themselves out of the running as custodial parents. Knowing that it is the task that is difficult and not the sex of the parent that makes the task difficult can help parents refocus on the reality of their situation and not assume they will have an easier time than their spouse (if they are female) or a harder time (if they are male). A realistic assessment of the demands of each parent's individual situation can lead to a better custody decision than reliance on the sex of the parent as the sole criterion. Such an assessment must include the relationship each parent has with the children as well as a wealth of other factors. (These factors range from the needs of the children to the time each parent will be able to spend with the children.)

One interesting approach, when joint custody is not viable, is to give custody to the parent who would allow the most contact between the children and the noncustodial parent.

Finally, we have to change our assumptions about the single parent to pave the way for greater role clarity for her or him. We have to help the single parent navigate through the pressures confronting him or her. When these strictures on the parents are removed, parents will be better able to go about their lives and reach their potentials.

3. *It is impossible to weigh whether single fathers or single mothers have an easier time adapting to single parenthood.*

Even though there are similarities between men and women with respect to which areas of parenting are found to be easy and which are difficult, there *are* differences between what mothers and fathers bring to their child-rearing experiences. Fathers have advantages in certain areas and disadvantages in others. On the plus side, the average single father has a higher income, more community support, greater permission to initiate dating, and more experience in the workplace than the average single mother. At the same time, he usually has less experience in housekeeping and in child care, and he may feel more out of place socially because he is a rarer commodity than the single mother.

There is no way to come up with an equation that accounts for the merits of each of these characteristics. If one believes money is the ultimate path to happiness, then fathers have an advantage. If one believes that having had more experience around the home, feeling a part of a larger social group, and not being a rare commodity are more important than income, then the mother has the advantage.

Adaptation depends on a complex interaction of variables that differ greatly from one individual to the next. No yardstick exists at this time with which to make a comparison based solely on sex.

4. *The importance of learning about single fathers' experiences is that more men will be willing to seek custody and more women will be willing to relinquish it.*

The inferences drawn from the findings of this study are that when more is learned about single fathers, other fathers will be encouraged to become more involved in all aspects of parenting. As mentioned, some fathers may be discouraged from seeking custody now because of a lack of information about the nature of the tasks. Fathers may be scared off from single parenting if they believe those who do it are extraordinary. When it is learned that fathers with custody are normal, average people who lived relatively traditional home lives before divorce and who have successfully negotiated many aspects of single parenting, other fathers may be encouraged to seek custody if they divorce. Fathers may be encouraged to get more involved in parenting if they do not have custody or if they are married. Learning more about the role of the single father brings fathering into a more realistic perspective. This makes it easier for a father to assess what he wants his involvement to be.

At the same time, the findings from the study should make it easier for mothers to relinquish custody. Many women feel guilty about even considering such a prospect. If they believed that only extraordinary men raise children alone and learn that this is a myth, they may be more willing to give up custody to their very ordinary ex-husband. Before, the mother might have worried that her husband would not make good single-father material. Knowing that the father does not need any outstanding characteristics to adapt to being a single parent will make it easier for her to believe the children will be well taken care of if she chooses to not raise them. In addition, mothers who learn that single mothers and fathers have the same types of problems with parenting will not feel they have to hold on to the children solely because of the myth that mothers make better parents. Incidentally, single mothers who learn about the similarities between themselves and fathers may put less pressure on themselves to be supermoms. If they see that *even* men cannot always happily juggle the demands of single parenting and work, they may feel more satisfied with their own situation.

*5. Such knowledge also will encourage both mothers and fathers to consider joint or shared custody.*

When both mothers and fathers learn what to expect realistically from single parenting, they will be better able to approach the issue of sharing custody. They will know what the demands are and where the stresses will lie for each of them. Two points from the study are particularly relevant here. First, fathers do better when the ex-wife is involved. This means fathers should be particularly interested in having the ex-wife stay involved, as that may ease the adjustment for all concerned. Second, fathers perform satisfactorily in many parenting areas when raising the children alone. This implies that mothers who worry about the competence of fathers should be encouraged by how satisfactorily the father functions and should move to let him do more parenting. Mothers should not have to worry that the father cannot cope with the demands of parenting, whether he has sole custody or is sharing it with her.

Learning about the expectations of single parenting may help the divorcing couple differentiate the issues that affect them as husband and wife from those that affect them as parents. Reducing the emotional content of their interactions may make it easier for them to work together toward joint custody or some other shared arrangement. This is not to say that joint custody is preferred in every case, only that it can be considered a viable option.

*6. Exploding the myths will help both children of divorce and children in the intact family.*

Although the focus of this book has been primarily on the fathers' experiences, it is vital to include some discussion of the impact on their children.

Learning about the fathers' successes and failures can influence the well-being of children. How fathers fare is related to how the children fare, and vice versa.

One of the major implications of this study is that if fathers learn more about single fathering and what it really entails, they will become more involved in all aspects of fathering. An increased involvement would bring the father into a less distant position in the family—a position that many fathers occupy. If the father becomes more central to the parenting tasks of the family, it will give him a different life experience. He may place less emphasis on his role as a worker. He will have more experiences with the people who are important to his family, such as friends, relatives, teachers, and neighbors. For better or worse, he will not have to defer to his wife as much on decisions concerning the children.

An increase in the father's involvement will mean a change for the mother. His involvement will free her from primary or sole responsibility for the day-to-day care of the children. She will be more able to explore other options for herself, which may result in increased income for the family, a different relationship between herself and the children, and a different relationship with her husband. Her relationships will have a greater chance of being built on choices and not on necessities.

Finally, the father's greater involvement in the family will mean more choices for the children. They will have two parents to relate to in a greater variety of ways. The father will be perceived by the child as being more competent as a parent. This sets up a cycle: As the father becomes more involved in parenting, he will feel more competent. As he feels more competent, his children will see him as more competent. The children seeing him as more competent will help the father to feel more competent and, in turn, will help the children to feel better about themselves.

If the parents are divorced, the children will have more options about which parent they can live with. Knowing the father has been an involved parent during the marriage gives them the option of choosing him as a primary parent.

If the noncustodial father stays more involved with the family after the divorce because he has a more realistic picture of single fathers, that will ease the children's adjustment.

Finally, if exposing the myths results in an increase in the number of fathers with custody, that will ease the transition of the children now living alone with their fathers. Their situation will not be so unusual.

Learning more about single fathering will encourage fathers to become involved or at least to make a better-reasoned decision about what they want their participation to be. Such involvement will ease the children's transition in the divorced family as well as improve parent-child relations in the intact family.

7. *Men's roles have shifted somewhat over the past decade. We are not moving quickly toward an androgynous society. Many men are changing in*

*reaction to the changes women are making. Fathers with custody have been pushed to change the most.*

Although the last decade has witnessed a greater appreciation by fathers of child rearing, a greater participation in it, and a greater sensitivity to women, there are few indications that men's roles have changed as dramatically as people might think. From this study, it was learned that even fathers who are on the cutting edge—those fathers who are raising their children alone—were not living radical life-styles before they gained custody. In most cases they were doing less housework and child care than their wives. It is only when most men *have* to change that they do so.

This is not to say that there are not nurturing men or fathers who are very involved in parenting. There always have been; they are found in every socioeconomic class and as members of every race. And there are more now than before. However, many fathers have not greatly changed their behavior over the years unless they have been thrown into a situation that put pressure on them to change.

What kind of role changes would signify a major shift for men in their behavior? First, it would mean a true sharing of the housework and child care in the intact family. From Blumstein and Schwartz (1983) and others, there is every indication that this is not the case. Yes, men are doing more—and in some cases a lot more. But women still carry the football. They may hand it off more often than before; but they are still the coaches, quarterbacks, and major shareholders of the team. Second, a major role change would occur if (in the same socioeconomic class) the percentage of working fathers with custody matched the percentage of working mothers with custody. Now, more fathers with custody work because they are less likely to be supported financially. Third, a major role change by men in our society would be a greater assault on the traditionally female-dominated professions, such as nursing and secretarial work. (A few telephone calls to nursing and secretarial schools in the Philadelphia area found that men are more highly represented than previously but are still a very small minority of the students in these fields. Contrast the minimal male assault on these professions with the female rush to medicine and law, where women now account for over one-third of the students.)[2] Finally, one would look for role changes in the social realm. Here there *is* evidence of change. The change, however, is engendered by women becoming more socially assertive, rather than men adopting new patterns of behavior that were self-generated. If any social changes are apparent in men, it is that they are becoming more socially cautious.

Thus we are not moving quickly toward a society in which sex roles have disappeared. Rather, we are moving toward one in which women are entering occupations that were traditionally male-dominated and a society in which men are doing a little more around the house—hardly a revolution for men. In fact, in relations between men and women, there appears to be some indication of a return to the old values. Sexual promiscuity is on the decline, in part as a result of the fear of communicable diseases. The buzzword of the 1980s is *commitment,* not *freedom* as it was in the late 1960s and 1970s.

There may be a male backlash to the women's movement. In the 1970s some men attempted to shed their macho behavior like an outgrown cocoon. They believed, correctly at the time, that many women wanted a new man. Now that nonsexist language has been institutionalized and men are more sensitive to the needs of women, some men wonder if they have lost something along the way, if they have become so-called wimps. Some men who changed to accommodate women are worried that something fundamentally male is missing, whether it is a playful macho image or a competitive zeal. Michael Norman (1984) addressed this issue in an article entitled "Standing His Ground." He wrote, "Yes, the male code needs reform. . . . But the fashion for reform, the drive to emasculate macho has produced a kind of numbing androgyny and has so blurred the lines of gender that I often find myself wanting to emulate women I know—bold, aggressive, vigorous role models" (p. 59).[3] I wonder how much more that is innately male men are going to give up.

Women, in turn, may not want men to give up anything else or change any more. If men become androgynous, it means that women give up something female, too. The sexes lose their complementarity. Femininity, like masculinity, is a central part of our culture. It is possible and desirable to have jobs open to women *and* to have men do more around the house without each sex losing a sense of self, of what is good about being male or female. Men can be more sensitive to women without losing what it means to be male.

The fathers who took part in this study have been placed in a nontraditional, typically female role. They have had to change. They have changed more than most divorced men in that their work lives, their home lives, and their social lives have all undergone a reordering of their priorities. These fathers do not behave the same way socially as they used to because of time demands. They do not emphasize success at work the way they used to. They appreciate being with their children more than they used to. If they did not have the opportunity to move into that role, however, they might never have seen that they had other choices in how to set priorities for themselves. Here again, it may be the change in the woman that causes the change in the man.

When these fathers move into the role of sole custodian, however, they do not lose all their male characteristics by any stretch of the imagination. Peter, in chapter 2, certainly did not. They handle the demands of parenting with a stiff-upper-lip mentality. This mentality is often associated with men who like actions to speak louder than words. They acknowledge that they may have some problems raising the children, but they go ahead and do it.

They do not readily admit to problems. Many feel uncomfortable asking for help. They are protective of their situation and see their assumption of the role of sole custodian more as a job or as their responsibility, not as a burden to complain about. They try to do the parenting as well as they can.

## The Potential

These fathers have broadened our perspective on fathering and mothering. They have shown that, with little previous experience, men can raise their children and be competent parents. Men have always had the capacity to do this, but until recently they never have had the chance. Men and women do a dance at home concerning the chores of parenting. She assumes she has to do most of them because he is incompetent. He willingly accepts this role. Given the opportunity, however, it has been shown that they each could do what the other was doing and still retain their own sexual identity.

The so-called new man will be around for awhile, but he is nothing special. For better or worse, he is just a slightly more flexible version of the old man. As fathers become more involved with children, there will be more choices for everyone. For men who have become custodial fathers, there is much to be encouraged about. Most of them feel satisfied that they are doing the right thing by raising their children. When men are pushed into parenting, they enjoy it. That is good news for everybody. When men start to push themselves, that will be even better news.

# Notes

## Chapter 1

1. Parsons and Bales (1955), and Crano and Aronoff (1981).
2. Hoferek (1982).
3. U.S. Department of Commerce (1984a).
4. Pear (1984).
5. U.S. Department of Commerce (1984b).
6. U.S. Department of Commerce (1983), based on figures for children living with all categories of single fathers.
7. U.S. Department of Commerce (1982), based on estimates in growth of numbers of working mothers.
8. U.S. Department of Commerce (1983).
9. Orthner, Brown, and Ferguson (1976); Katz (1979).
10. Derdeyn (1976a).
11. Ibid.; Polikoff (1982).
12. Trattner (1979).
13. Derdeyn (1976a), Roman and Haddad (1978), and Santrock and Warshak (1979).
14. Bowlby (1951).
15. Orthner, Brown, and Ferguson (1976).
16. Atkinson (1984).
17. Ibid.
18. Nuta (1983).
19. Bartz and Witcher (1978).
20. Rank and LeCroy (1983) speak of the use of multiple perspectives.
21. For readings on a feminist perspective, see Berlin and Kravetz (1981), McIntyre (1981), and Bograd (1984).
22. For readings on the life-cycle perspective, see Rhodes (1977) and Walsh (1982).
23. For readings on role ambiguity, see Sarbin and Allen (1968) and Van Sell, Brief, and Schuler (1981).
24. For readings on coping and adaptation, see Coelho, Hamburg, and Adams (1974).
25. For a view of this point, read Minuchin's comments in Simon (1984b).

26. For some recent articles on these issues and others of similar interest, see Krause (1983), Atkinson (1984), and Schwartz (1984). Also see recent editions of the journal *Family Law Quarterly*.

For further information on the demographics of marital instability, see Spanier and Glick (1981).

For further information on the impact of divorce on income, see Weiss (1984).

## Chapter 2

1. The description of "growing up a little faster" that appears in the chapter to describe what Keith experienced being raised in a single parent family is a phrase also used by Weiss (1979).

## Chapter 3

1. Brody (1983). Copyright © 1983 by The New York Times Company. Reprinted by permission.
2. Goode (1956); Zeiss, Zeiss, and Johnson (1980).
3. See Wallerstein and Kelly (1980), G.L. Greif (1984b), and Schwartz (1984).
4. The reader is again referred to recent articles by Krause (1983), Atkinson (1984), and Schwartz (1984).
5. Atkinson (1984).
6. For other results, see Chang and Deinard (1982) and Orthner, Brown, and Ferguson (1976).
7. Fathers who won custody in court were also looked at separately. No significant differences were found.

## Chapter 4

1. Pleck and Corfman (1979) and Maret and Finlay (1984).
2. G.L. Greif (1983a).
3. U.S. Department of Commerce (1976).
4. Blank (1984).

For further information on men and housework, see Clarke-Stewart (1977), and Lein (1979), and for daycare, see Turner and Smith (1983).

## Chapter 5

1. For research on fathers' work experiences, see Gasser and Taylor (1976), Keshet and Rosenthal (1976), Mendes (1976b), and Chang and Deinard (1982). Orthner, Brown, and Ferguson (1976) and Smith and Smith (1981) reported no problems for fathers at work.

## Chapter 6

1. Clarke-Stewart (1977).
2. Lynn (1974).
3. Rutter (1972), Lamb and Lamb (1976), Levine (1976), Parke and Sarovin (1976), and Rendina and Dickerscheid (1976).
4. Keshet and Rosenthal (1976), Mendes (1976b), Orthner, Brown, and Ferguson (1976), and Bartz and Witcher (1978).
5. Derdeyn (1976b).
6. Atkinson (1984) connects this approach to deciding custody with the tender-years presumption.
7. Wallerstein and Kelly (1980) and Moles (1982).

For other information on children's adjustment, see Ellison (1983).

For information on joint custody, see J.B. Greif (1979).

## Chapter 7

1. White and Bloom (1981).
2. See Gasser and Taylor (1976), Keshet and Rosenthal (1976), Orthner, Brown, and Ferguson (1976), Bartz and Witcher (1978), and Chang and Deinard (1982).
3. For other research on the difficulties following divorce, see Wallerstein and Kelly (1980) Smith and Smith (1981). For difficulties faced by the divorced father, see Jacobs (1982), Pichitino (1983), and Tepp (1983).
4. Some fathers who were telephoned to be interviewed one to two years after completing the survey had remarried.

## Chapter 8

1. Fischer and Cardea (1981), Fischer and Cardea (1982), and Fischer (1983) have all examined mothers without custody living in and around Texas. Todres (1978) studied mothers without custody living in Canada.
2. DeFrain and Eirick (1981), in a study comparing custodial fathers with custodial mothers, noted that fathers were more apt to feed negative information to the children about the absent spouse than were mothers.
3. See, for example, Wallerstein and Kelly (1980).

## Chapter 9

1. Polikoff (1982), and Woods, Been, and Schulman (198⌐,
2. Cassety (1982, 1984).
3. Molinoff (1977).
4. Associated Press (1983).
5. Pear (1984).
6. For more information, see Krause (1983).

## Chapter 10

For comparative information, see Bloom and Caldwell (1981) who compare the adjustment of men and women during separation.

## Chapter 11

1. U.S Department of Commerce (1983).
2. For more information on children and divorce, see Santrock and Warshak (1979), Wallerstein and Kelly (1980), Wallerstein (1983, 1984), Hetherington, Cox, and Cox (1979), Ambert (1982, 1984), Bronkowski, Bequette, and Boomhower (1984), and Woody, Colley, Schlegelmilch, Maginn, and Balsanek (1984).

## Chapter 12

1. For further elaboration on this theory, see Van Sell, Brief, and Schuler (1981).
2. Lin (1984).
3. Norman (1984). Copyright © 1984 by The New York Times Company. Reprinted by permission.

For other information on fathers with custody, see George and Wilding (1972), Brown and Stones (1979), and Nieto (1982).

For more information on strategies, see Weltner (1982).

For other information on sex roles, see Pleck and Pleck (1980), Brownmiller (1984), and Simon (1984a).

# Appendix

The study was supported by grants from two foundations that wish to remain anonymous. The study fulfilled the dissertation requirement for a Doctor of Social Welfare degree at the Columbia University School of Social Work.

The open-ended responses were coded by six different people after they were trained by the author. The data were then keypunched and placed in the computer. The SPSS package was used for analysis of the data. Tables A–1 through A–15 show the relevant demographic data gathered and analyzed.

Seven variables were hypothesized to have an impact on these fathers' experiences.

1. *The age of the children being raised.* It was hypothesized that fathers raising older children would have an easier time in a number of areas. First, these children would not need much physical child care. An inexperienced father, it was believed, would have difficulties with diapering, feeding, bathing, and arranging child care for very young children. Older children would not impose those time requirements. Second, older children would be able to take care of themselves after school, thus freeing the father from worrying about their well-being. Third, it was believed that older children would be able to help around the house more, further easing the father's transition.

The issue of the age of the children was a difficult one to explore. Using the mean age of all of the children being raised by a particular father might not have been helpful in understanding the father's parenting demands. A father raising a very young child—say, a three-year-old—and a fifteen-year-old would be shown to have a child at an average age of nine. The demands of raising a nine-year-old, however, are different from those of raising a fifteen-year-old, who could help out around the home, or a three-year-old, who would need constant watching.

Therefore, the fathers were grouped by the ages of the children being raised in the following way: fathers raising one- to four-year-olds, a preschool group who would need constant supervision; fathers raising five-to eleven-year-olds, a group who would be in school during the day but might need supervision after school; and fathers raising twelve- to eighteen-year-olds, a group of children who could supervise themselves and do a good deal of the housework and cooking if needed. This approach resulted in the following groupings: fathers with one- to four-year-olds = 48 (4.2 percent); fathers with five- to eleven-year-olds = 304 (26.7 percent); and fathers raising twelve- to eighteen-year-olds = 508 (44.7 percent). This approach removed 25 percent of the men from the sample. For instance, fathers raising a child under five and a child over five were excluded, as were fathers raising three children with ages in each of the different groups. It also meant that there was a small group, the fathers with the youngest children, that was being compared with two larger groups, a statistical weakness. For these reasons, the results from these comparisons should be looked at only in terms of possible trends.

2. *The sex of the children being raised.* It was believed that sons would be easier for men to raise. Because the courts have often favored the mother's having custody of daughters, and because some research has supported the notion that children do better when raised by the same-sex single parent, it was thought this pattern would repeat. With daughters, fathers would be unsure about how to explain sexuality, how to buy dresses, and how to deal with a lack of a female role model in the home.

For analysis, fathers were grouped by whether they were raising only girls, only boys, or both boys and girls. This approach yielded the following group sizes: fathers raising only girls = 288 (25 percent); fathers raising only boys = 482 (42 percent); and fathers raising both boys and girls = 366 (32 percent).

3. *The number of children being raised.* It was hypothesized that the fewer the children being raised, the easier the father's adjustment would be. Having to raise a number of children would mean more feelings to be dealt with, more child-care arrangements to be made, and more unforeseen crises that could arise.

4. *The income of the father.* A high salary was perceived as being connected to the ability to purchase more services to help with the child rearing and housekeeping. It was also thought that a greater income would be related to more freedom on the job, the ability to set one's own schedule, and more freedom to socialize in the manner the father desired.

5. *The number of years of sole custody.* It was hypothesized that as time went on, single parenting would get easier. Experience would pay off for the father in all areas of parenting.

6. *The involvement of the ex-wife.* As mentioned in the first chapter, it was believed that fathers whose ex-wives were involved with the children would have an easier time adjusting because they would have more assistance and because the children would not be suffering from separation from their mother.

To analyze the impact of the mother's involvement, the responses to the question, "How involved is your ex-wife with the children?" were used. The

responses were grouped so that 7 percent described their ex-wife as very involved, 73 percent as somewhat or slightly involved, and 20 percent as not at
all involved. This resulted in three different, though uneven, groups of
fathers with which the impact of the ex-wife's involvement could be explored.

7. *Whether the father wanted custody.* As Mendes (1976a) has pointed
out, fathers who sought custody adjusted better than fathers who had
custody thrust upon them against their wishes. It was believed that the fathers
in this study who said they wanted to be sole custodians would adjust more
easily to the demands of parenting than would the fathers who were forced
into that role by the mother's abdication.

The different areas that it was believed a father would have to deal with
in order to make an adequate adjustment to being a single parent are:

1. Running the home, which includes the physical maintenance of the house
   and taking care of the children.
2. Balancing the demands of work while child rearing.
3. Establishing a satisfying relationship with the children being raised.
4. Adjusting to being single and feeling comfortable socializing.
5. Establishing a satisfactory relationship with the ex-wife vis-à-vis her involvement with the children.

A sixth area also emerged from the follow-up interviews as being one of great
importance to the fathers. This area dealt with the father's struggles with the
legal aspect of being a single father.

Multiple regression equations were run to determine which variables had
the best ability to predict comfort and satisfaction. Income, or feeling financially comfortable, proved to be the best predictor (Greif 1983c). All other
comparisons discussed in the book were significant at $p < .05$.

## Limitations

As with most studies, there are a number of limitations to the approach that
was used. Ideally, when one is doing a study, a sample should be gained that
is considered representative of the population being studied. In the case of
single fathers, this would require having a national listing of all fathers with
custody and drawing a representative sample from that group and asking
them to complete a questionnaire. No such national list is available. Using
court records of men who have been granted custody by the courts is costly
and time consuming, cannot easily be done on a national basis, and will only
produce a sample of fathers who have gone through the courts. Many men
are raising their children because of agreements they have reached with their
wives without going through the court system.

Because the approach used in this research is based on a survey that was published in a magazine for members of PWP, the sample is not representative of all single fathers in the United States for a number of reasons:

1. The fathers in the survey were members of a self-help group.
2. These fathers chose to answer the questionnaire; they are a self-selected sample. Nothing is known about the fathers who did not choose to answer the questionnaire. Hence it is not know whether the respondents are better adjusted to their role and wanted to answer the questionnaire, perhaps to prove a point, or are not as well adjusted and needed to respond to make their story known.
3. These fathers may have given socially desirable answers to improve people's view of them. When people take part in a study, if they have a point they wish to make—for example, if the fathers wanted their ex-wives to know how well they were doing—they might improve their answers to give a better impression of themselves. For example, child and wife abuse were never admitted to by any of the fathers.
4. Because PWP does not possess a list of all their single fathers with custody, it is impossible to know what compelled some fathers to answer the questionnaires and others not to respond. No follow-up could be done to include the other fathers or to learn why they did not complete the questionnaire.

Another limitation is that, because only the fathers were surveyed, the systemic nature of the relationship with the children and the mother could not be examined. Studying all members of the family may have produced different results.

Given these limitations, a number of points need to be made about the benefits of the approach that was used. As mentioned, there was little information about this group of fathers available. The studies that had been completed had similar sampling problems. This study drew a much larger sample size, which meant that certain statistical methods, though not truly applicable to a nonrandomized or nonrepresentative sample, could be used to look at possible trends in the population. This was also a national sample. Unlike other research, which usually has come from one region or one city, this sample includes responses from forty-eight states and Canada. This means there is a greater opportunity for diversity in the sample. Finally, the chance to use information drawn both from a sample and from interviews permits two kinds of looks at these fathers. Trends among the fathers could be examined as well as the individual stories. The interviews provided an opportunity to cross-check the information gained from the questionnaires to see how valid the responses were in capturing the fathers' experiences. Even though the interviews were primarily conducted on the East Coast, no regional differences were found in the results.

With these limitations and benefits, it is best for the reader to think of these findings as possible trends in what single fathers with children are experiencing.

**Table A–1**
**Racial Composition of the Sample**

| Race | Absolute Frequency | Adjusted Frequency (%) |
|------|--------------------|------------------------|
| White | 1,070 | 97.4 |
| Black | 7 | 0.6 |
| Oriental | 2 | 0.2 |
| Hispanic | 7 | 0.6 |
| Other | 10 | 0.9 |
| No response | 40 | — |
| | 1,136 | 100.0 |

**Table A–2**
**Financial Background of the Sample**

| Income of Fathers | Absolute Frequency | Cumulative Frequency (%) |
|-------------------|--------------------|--------------------------|
| $10,000 | 13 | 3.6 |
| $15,000 | 32 | 11.3 |
| $20,000 | 78 | 27.0 |
| $25,000 | 100 | 49.9 |
| $30,000 | 119 | 69.4 |
| $35,000 | 53 | 79.6 |
| $40,000 | 59 | 88.7 |
| $45,000 | 13 | 91.3 |
| $50,000 | 43 | 96.4 |

Note: $n = 1,093$; mean = $28,325; mode = $30,000 (mode $n = 119$); median = $25,992; minimum = $5,000 (if figure is given); maximum = $115,000.

**Table A–3**
**Occupational Background of the Sample**

| Code Number | Occupational Equivalent | Absolute Frequency | Cumulative Frequency (%) |
|---|---|---|---|
| 34 | Salesman and sales clerk | 49 | 12.7 |
| 40 | Carpenter, millwright, pressman | 33 | 21.9 |
| 41 | Engraver, buyer and shipper, photographer, plumber | 48 | 26.4 |
| 42 | Tool and die maker, advertising agent, and salesman of advertising | 41 | 30.2 |
| 44 | Fireman, telegraph operator | 26 | 33.9 |
| 47 | Insurance agent, health technologists, chemical and and mechanical technician | 127 | 47.7 |
| 48 | Purchasing agents and buyers, bookkeepers, and machinists | 49 | 52.2 |
| 50 | Managers, administrators, supervisors | 141 | 67.0 |
| 51 | Stock brokers and computer programmers | 68 | 73.4 |
| 67 | Chemical and other engineers | 87 | 92.1 |

Notes: Using Occupational Classification Scale—10 most frequent codes. $n = 1,127$; mean (without 0 codes) = 48.9; mode = 50; median = 48; minimum = 0; maximum = 82, 0 code was used for students, unemployed, and retired responses. 82 code is for physicians.


**Table A–4**
**Educational Background of the Sample**

| Highest Number of Years of Education Completed | Absolute Frequency | Adjusted Frequency (%) |
|---|---|---|
| 12 = high school | 333 | 29.8 |
| 14 | 159 | 14.2 |
| 16 = college | 247 | 22.1 |
| 18 | 150 | 13.4 |
| 20 = doctorate | 40 | 3.6 |

Note: $n = 1,117$; mean = 14.6; mode = 12 (mode $n = 333$); median = 14.2.

## Table A–5
## Regional Background of the Sample
*(states with 25 respondents or more)*

| States | Absolute Frequency | Adjusted Frequency (%) |
|---|---|---|
| California | 152 | 13.4 |
| Florida | 27 | 2.4 |
| Illinois | 36 | 3.2 |
| Iowa | 26 | 2.3 |
| Maryland | 66 | 5.8 |
| Michigan | 65 | 5.7 |
| Minnesota | 35 | 3.1 |
| Ohio | 74 | 6.5 |
| New Jersey | 37 | 3.2 |
| New York | 74 | 6.5 |
| North Carolina | 31 | 2.7 |
| Pennsylvania | 59 | 5.2 |
| Texas | 46 | 4.0 |
| Virginia | 58 | 5.1 |
| Washington | 41 | 3.6 |

Notes: $n = 1,134$; mode – California (mode $n = 152$); Responses came from every state except Alaska and Wyoming; 18 responses were received from Canada.

## Table A–6
## Number of Miles Ex-Wife Lives from Father

| Number of Miles | Absolute Frequency | Cumulative Frequency (%) |
|---|---|---|
| 5 | 80 | 25.3 |
| 10 | 104 | 40.7 |
| 20 | 43 | 52.7 |
| 30 | 28 | 58.1 |
| 50 | 16 | 63.2 |
| 100 | 15 | 68.4 |
| 150 | 14 | 71.7 |
| 300 | 15 | 76.2 |
| 1,000 | 25 | 86.4 |
| 1,500 | 25 | 91.4 |

Note: $n = 1,098$; mean = 398; mode = 10 (mode $n = 104$); median = 19.8.

## Table A–7
## Religious Background of the Sample

| Religion | Absolute Frequency | Adjusted Frequency (%) |
|---|---|---|
| Jewish | 51 | 4.7 |
| Protestant | 451 | 41.3 |
| Catholic | 250 | 22.9 |
| Other | 116 | 10.6 |
| No preference/none | 222 | 20.3 |
| No response | 46 | — |
| | 1,136 | 100.0 |

## Table A–8
## Age of Father

| Age | Absolute Frequency | Cumulative Frequency (%) |
|---|---|---|
| 25 | 3 | 0.9 |
| 30 | 22 | 1.9 |
| 35 | 50 | 24.0 |
| 40 | 73 | 53.3 |
| 45 | 47 | 80.0 |
| 50 | 19 | 93.3 |

Note: $n = 1,133$; mean = 40.1; mode = 39 (mode $n = 84$); median = 39.9; minimum = 22; maximum = 65.

## Table A–9
## Age of Mother

| Age | Absolute Frequency | Cumulative Frequency (%) |
|---|---|---|
| 25 | 14 | 3.5 |
| 30 | 37 | 15.7 |
| 35 | 74 | 41.7 |
| 40 | 67 | 73.7 |
| 45 | 25 | 91.9 |
| 50 | 5 | 98.4 |

Note: $n = 1,132$; mean = 36.7; mode = 36 (mode $n = 86$); median = 36.6; minimum = 19; maximum = 57.

## Table A–10
## Year of Marriage

| Year | Absolute Frequency | Cumulative Frequency (%) |
|------|--------------------|--------------------------|
| 1955 | 2 | 3.8 |
| 1960 | 37 | 17.1 |
| 1965 | 65 | 48.9 |
| 1970 | 47 | 78.5 |
| 1975 | 18 | 95.6 |
| 1980 | 1 | 100.0 |

Note: $n$ = 1,131; mean = 65.7; mode = 67 (mode $n$ = 84); median = 65.7; minimum = 48; maximum = 80.

## Table A–11
## Year of Separation or Divorce

| Year | Absolute Frequency | Cumulative Frequency (%) |
|------|--------------------|--------------------------|
| 1970 | 14 | 3.0 |
| 1975 | 53 | 18.4 |
| 1977 | 84 | 33.4 |
| 1979 | 141 | 58.4 |
| 1981 | 195 | 96.6 |

Note: $n$ = 1,126; mean = 78.0; mode = 80 (mode $n$ = 202); median = 78.8; minimum = 65; maximum = 82.

## Table A–12
## Years of Sole Custody

| Number of Years | Absolute Frequency | Cumulative Frequency (%) |
|-----------------|--------------------|--------------------------|
| 1 | 244 | 23.0 |
| 2 | 257 | 47.3 |
| 3 | 130 | 59.6 |
| 4 | 137 | 72.5 |
| 5 | 88 | 80.8 |
| 10 | 16 | 96.5 |

Note: $n$ = 1,058; mean = 3.58; mode = 2 (mode $n$ = 257); median = 2.7; minimum = 1; maximum = 16.

## Table A–13
**Age Range of Children Eighteen and Under with Father**

| Age | Absolute Frequency | Combined Group Adjusted Frequency |
|---|---|---|
| 1 | 7 | |
| 2 | 28 | 1 – 4 = 5.8% |
| 3 | 37 | |
| 4 | 58 | |
| 5 | 79 | |
| 6 | 91 | |
| 7 | 100 | |
| 8 | 118 | 5 – 11 = 39.2% |
| 9 | 117 | |
| 10 | 127 | |
| 11 | 146 | |
| 12 | 175 | |
| 13 | 186 | |
| 14 | 149 | |
| 15 | 138 | 12 – 18 = 55% |
| 16 | 178 | |
| 17 | 160 | |
| 18 | 102 | |
| | 1996 | |

Note: Mean = 11.6; mode = 13 (mode *n* = 186); median = 12.

## Table A–14
**Age Range of Children Eighteen and Under Being Raised Elsewhere**

| Age | Absolute Frequency | Combined Group Adjusted Frequency |
|---|---|---|
| 1 | 7 | |
| 2 | 4 | 1 – 4 = 8.4% |
| 3 | 10 | |
| 4 | 4 | |
| 5 | 7 | |
| 6 | 8 | |
| 7 | 9 | |
| 8 | 10 | 5 – 11 = 28.8% |
| 9 | 18 | |
| 10 | 17 | |
| 11 | 16 | |
| 12 | 22 | |
| 13 | 29 | |
| 14 | 23 | |
| 15 | 20 | 12 – 18 = 62.7% |
| 16 | 25 | |
| 17 | 27 | |
| 18 | 39 | |
| | 295 | |

Note: Mean = 12.2; mode = 18 (mode *n* = 39); median = 13.

**Table A–15**
**What Job Changes Have You Experienced Due to Being a Single Parent?**
**(Check All That Apply.)**

| | |
|---|---|
| 130 | Bringing work home |
| 364 | Reducing travel |
| 212 | Reducing work load |
| 254 | Working flexible hours |
| 381 | Having to miss work |
| 395 | Arriving late/leaving early |
| 211 | Taking new job/changing job |
| 102 | Taking on additional work |
| 43 | Being fired |
| 66 | Quitting |
| 303 | None of the above |

Note: $n = 1,134$; missing data account for the response rate being lower than the total sample size.

# References and Related Bibliography

Ambert, A. 1982. Differences in children's behavior toward custodial mothers and fathers. *Journal of Marriage and the Family* 44 (1): 73–86.

————. 1984. Longitudinal changes in children's behavior toward custodial parents. *Journal of Marriage and the Family* 46 (2): 463–467.

Associated Press, 1983. Child support pay lags, study finds. *San Diego Union*, July 7: 16.

Atkinson, J. 1984. Criteria for deciding child custody in the trial and appellate courts. *Family Law Quarterly* 28 (1): 1–42.

Bartz, K.W., and Witcher, W.C. 1978. When father gets custody. *Children Today* 7 (5): 2–6, 35.

Berlin, S., and Kravetz, D. 1981. Women as victims: A feminist social work perspective. *Social Work* 26 (6): 447–449.

Blank, H. 1984. Testimony of the Children's Defense Fund before the Subcommittee on Elementary, Secondary, and Vocational Education of the Educational and Labor Committee, April 30.

Bloom, B.L., and Caldwell, R.A. 1981. Sex differences in adjustment during the process of marital separation. *Journal of Marriage and the Family* 43 (3): 693–701.

Blumstein, P., and Schwartz, P. 1983. *American couples.* New York: William Morrow.

Bograd, M. 1984. Family systems approaches to wife battering: A feminist critique. *American Journal of Orthopsychiatry* 54 (4): 558–568.

Bonkowski, S.E.; Bequette, S.Q.; and Boomhower, S. 1984. A group design to help children adjust to parental divorce. *Social Casework* 65 (3): 131–137.

Bowlby, J. 1951. *Maternal care and mental health.* Geneva: World Health Organization.

Brody, J.E. 1983. Divorce's stress exacts long-term health toll. *The New York Times,* December 13: C1, 5.

Brown, A., and Stones, C. 1979. A group for lone fathers. *Social Work Today* 47 (10): 3–7.

Brownmiller, S. 1984. *Femininity.* New York: Linden Press/Simon and Schuster.

Cassety, J. 1982. Child support: New focus for social work practice. *Social Work* 27 (6): 504–508.

————. 1984. Child support: Emerging issues for practice. *Social Casework* 65 (2): 74–80.

Chang, P., and Deinard, A.S. 1982. Single-father caretakers: Demographic characteristics and adjustment processes. *American Journal of Orthopsychiatry* 52 (2): 236–242.

Clarke-Stewart, A. 1977. *Child care in the family*. New York: Academic Press.

Coelho, G.V.; Hamburg, D.A.; and Adams, J.E. (editors) 1972. *Coping and Adaptation*. New York: Basic Books.

Crano, W.D., and Aronoff, J. 1981. A cross-cultural study of expressive and instrumental role complementarity in the family. *American Sociological Review 43* (4): 463–471.

DeFrain, J., and Eirick, R. 1981. Coping as divorced single parents: A comparative study of fathers and mothers. *Family Relations 30* (2): 265–273.

Derdeyn, A.P. 1976a. Child custody contests in historical perspective. *American Journal of Psychiatry 11* (12): 1369–1375.

——— . 1976b. A consideration of legal issues in child custody contests. *Archives of General Psychiatry 33* (2): 163–167.

Ellison, E.S. 1983. Issues concerning parental harmony and children's psychosocial adjustment. *American Journal of Orthopsychiatry 53* (1): 73–80.

*Family Law Reporter.* 1982. "Custody—Tender Years Presumption" (*Chastain* v. *Chastain*), Vol. 8, 2261, 3-9-82; and "Custody—Tender Years Presumption—Suicide Attempts" (*Leisge* v. *Leisge*), Vol. 8, 2250, 7-27-82.

Fischer, J.L. 1983. Mothers living apart from their children. *Family Relations 32* (3): 351–357.

Fischer, J., and Cardea, J.M. 1981. Mothers living apart from their children. *Alternative Lifestyles 4* (2): 218–227.

——— . 1982. Mother-child relationships of mothers living apart from their children. *Alternative Lifestyles 5* (1): 42–53.

Friedan, B. 1977. *The Feminine Mystique*. New York: Dell Books.

Furstenberg, F.F.; Nord, C.W.; Peterson, J.L.; and Zill, N. 1983. The life course of children of divorce: Marital disruption and parental contact. *American Sociological Review 48* (5): 656–668.

Gasser, R.D., and Taylor, C.M. 1976. Role adjustment of single parent fathers with dependent children. *The Family Coordinator 25* (4): 397–401.

George, V., and Wilding, P. 1972. *Motherless families*. London: Routledge and Kegan Paul.

Gersick, K. 1979. Fathers by choice: Divorced men who receive custody of their children. In G. Levinger and D.C. Moles, eds., *Divorce and separation*. New York: Basic Books.

Goode, W.S. 1956. *After divorce*. Glencoe, Ill.: Free Press.

Greer, G. 1971. *The Female Eunuch*. New York: McGraw-Hill.

Greif, G.L. 1982. Dads raising kids. *The Single Parent 25* (9): 17–23.

——— . 1983a. A report on fathers whose wives died. Paper presented at the Sixth Annual Conference of the Forum for Death Education and Counseling, October.

——— . 1983b. Widowers. *The Single Parent 26* (7): 29–32.

——— . 1983c. Single fathers raising children following separation and divorce. D.S.W. diss., Columbia University School of Social Work.

——— . 1984a. Custodial dads and their ex-wives. *The Single Parent 27* (1).

——— . 1984b. The pros and cons to the custodial father of the noncustodial mother's involvement with the children. Paper presented at the National Council on Family Relations Convention, October.

———— . 1985a. Children and housework in the single father family. *Family Relations* 34 (3): 353–357.

———— . 1985b. Practice with single fathers. *Social Work in Education* 7 (4): 231–243.

———— . 1985c. Single fathers rearing children. *Journal of Marriage and the Family* 47 (1): 185–191.

———— . In press. Mothers without custody. *Social Work.*

Greif, J.B. 1979. Fathers, children, and joint custody. *American Journal of Orthopsychiatry* 49 (2): 311–319.

Hetherington, E.M.; Cox, M.; and Cox, R. 1976. Divorced fathers. *The Family Coordinator* 25 (4): 417–428.

———— . 1979. The development of the children in mother-headed families. In D. Reiss and H. Hoffman, eds., *The American family.* New York: Plenum Press.

Hoferek, M.J. 1982. Sex-role prescriptions and attitudes of physical educators. *Sex Roles* 8 (1): 83–98.

Jacobs, J.W. 1982. The effect of divorce on fathers: An overview of the literature. *American Journal of Psychiatry* 139 (10): 1235–1241.

Katz, A.J. 1979. Lone fathers: Perspectives and implications for family policy. *The Family Coordinator* 28 (4): 521–528.

Kesher, H.F., and Rosenthal, K.N. 1976. Single parent families: A new study. *Children Today* 7 (3): 13–17.

Krause, H.D. 1977. *Family law in a nutshell.* Minneapolis: West.

———— . 1983. Reflections on child support. *Family Law Quarterly* 27 (2): 109–132.

Lamb, M.E., and Lamb, J. 1976. The nature and importance of the father-infant relationship. *The Family Coordinator* 25 (4): 379–385.

Lein, L. 1979. Male participation in home life: Impact of social supports and breadwinner responsibility on the allocation of tasks. *The Family Coordinator* 28 (5): 489–495.

Levine, J. 1976. *Who will raise the children.* New York: Bantam Books.

Lin, J. 1984. Women are finding their way into a man's world. *Philadelphia Inquirer,* October 1: C1, 3.

Lynn, D.B. 1974. *The father: His role in child development.* Monterey, Calif., Brooks Cole.

McIntyre, K. 1981. Role of mothers in father–daughter incest: A feminist analysis. *Social Work* 26 (6): 462–466.

Maret, E., and Finlay, B. 1984. The distribution of household labor among women in dual-earner families. *Journal of Marriage and the Family* 46 (2): 357–364.

Mendes, H. 1976a. Single fatherhood. *Social Work* 21 (4): 308–312.

———— . 1976b. Single fathers. *The Family Coordinator* 25 (4): 439–444.

Moles, D.C. 1982. Trends in divorce and effects on children. Paper presented at the meetings of the American Academy for the Advancement of Science, Washington, D.C.

Molinoff, D.D. 1977. Father's Day. *The New York Times,* May 22: 13–17.

Nieto, D.S. 1982. Aiding the single father. *Social Work* 27 (6): 473–478.

Norman, M. 1984. Standing his ground. *New York Times Magazine,* April 1: 55.

Nuta, V.R. 1983. Single parents hardest hit by unemployment. *The Single Parent* 26 (1): 9–10.

Orthner, D.K.; Brown, T.; and Ferguson, D. 1976. Single parent fatherhood: An emerging lifestyle. *The Family Coordinator 25* (4): 429–437.

Parke, R., and Sarovin, D.B. 1976. The father's role in infancy: A re-evaluation. *The Family Coordinator 25* (4): 365–371.

Parsons, T., and Bales, R. 1955. *Family, socialization, and interaction processes.* Glencoe, Ill.: Free Press.

Pear, R. 1984. Wage lag is found for white women. *The New York Times*, January 16: A1, B10.

Pichitino, J.P. 1983. Profile of the single father: A thematic integration of the literature. *Personnel and Guidance Journal 9* (1): 295–299.

Pleck, E., and Pleck, J.H. 1980. *The American man.* Englewood Cliffs, N.J.: Prentice-Hall.

Pleck, J., and Corfman, E. 1979. Married men: Work and family. In E. Corfman, ed., *Families today*, Vol. 1. Washington, D.C.: U.S. Department of Health, Education and Welfare.

Polikoff, N. 1982. Why are mothers losing: A brief analysis of criteria used in child custody determinations. *Women's Rights Law Reporter 7* (3): 235–243.

———. 1984. Fathers rarely *ask* for custody. *The Washington Post*, November 10: A21.

Rank, M., and LeCroy, C. 1983. Toward a multiple perspective in family theory and practice: The case of social exchange theory, symbolic interactionism, and conflict theory. *Family Relations 32* (3): 441–448.

Rendina, I., and Dickerscheid, J. 1976. Father involvement with first born infants. *The Family Coordinator 25* (4): 373–378.

Rhodes, S. 1977. A developmental approach to the life cycle of the family. *Social Casework 58* (5): 301–311.

Roman, M., and Haddad, W. 1978. *The disposable parents: The case for joint custody.* London: Penguin.

Rosenthal, K.M., and Keshet, H.F. 1981. *Fathers without partners.* Totowa, N.J.: Rowman and Littlefield.

Rutter, M. 1972. *Maternal deprivation reassessed.* Baltimore: Penguin.

Santrock, J.W., and Warshak, R.A. 1979. Father custody and social development in boys and girls. *Journal of Social Issues 35* (4): 112–125.

Sarbin, T.R., and Allen, V.L. 1968. Role theory. In G. Lindzey and E. Aronson, eds., *The handbook of social psychology*, Vol. 1, 2nd ed. Reading, Mass.: Addison-Wesley.

Schwartz, S.F.G. 1984. Toward a presumption of joint custody. *Family Law Quarterly 28* (2): 225–246.

Simon, R. 1984a. From ideology to practice: The Women's Project in Family Therapy. *Family Therapy Networker 8* (3): 29–32, 38–40.

———. 1984b. Stranger in a strange land: An interview with Salvador Minuchin. *Family Therapy Networker 8* (6): 20–31, 66–68.

Smith, R.M., and Smith, C.W. 1981. Child-rearing and single parent fathers. *Family Relations 30* (3): 411–417.

Spanier, G.B., and Glick, P.C. 1981. Marital instability in the United States: Some correlates and recent changes. *Family Relations 30* (3): 329–335.

Tepp, A.V. 1983. Divorced fathers: Predictors of continued parental involvement. *American Journal of Psychiatry 140* (11): 1465–1469.

Terkel, S. 1974. *Working.* New York: Pantheon.

Todres, R. 1978. Runaway wives: An increasing North American phenomenon. *The Family Coordinator 27* (1): 17–21.

Trattner, W.I. 1979. *From poor law to welfare state.* New York: Free Press.

Turner, P.H., and Smith, R.M. 1983. Single parents and day care. *Family Relations 32* (2): 215–226.

U.S. Department of Commerce, Bureau of the Census. 1976. Population characteristics. Series P-20, No. 298, October.

——— . 1982. Characteristics of American youth and children: 1980. Series P-23, No. 114, January.

——— . 1983. Marital status and living arrangements: March 1982. Series P-20, No. 380, May.

——— . 1984a. Earnings in 1981 of married-couple families, by selected characteristics of husbands and wives. Series P-23, No. 133.

——— . 1984b. Household and family characteristics: March 1983. Series P-20, No. 388, May.

Van Sell, M.; Brief, A.P.; and Schuler, R.S. 1981. Role conflict and ambiguity: Integration of the literature and directions for future research. *Human Relations 34* (1): 43–71.

Wallerstein, J. 1983. Children of divorce: The psychological tasks of the child. *American Journal of Orthopsychiatry 53* (2): 230–243.

——— . 1984. Paper presented at the 1984 American Orthopsychiatric Convention. Reported in *Psychology Today 18* (7): 9.

Wallerstein, J., and Kelly, J. 1980. *Surviving the Breakup.* New York: Basic Books.

Walsh, F., ed. 1982. *Normal family processes.* New York: Guilford Press.

Weiss, R.S. 1976. The emotional impact of marital separation. *Journal of Social Issues 32* (1): 135–145.

——— . 1979. Growing up a little faster: The experiences of growing up in a single-parent household. *Journal of Social Issues 35* (4): 97–111.

——— . 1984. The impact of marital dissolution on income and consumption in single-parent households. *Journal of Marriage and the Family 46* (1): 115–127.

Weltner, J.S. 1982. A structural approach to the single parent family. *Family Process 21* (4): 203–210.

White, S.L., and Bloom, B. 1981. Factors related to the adjustment of divorcing men. *Family Relations 30* (3): 349–360.

Woods, L.; Been, V.; and Schulman, J. 1982. The use of sex and economic discriminatory criteria in child custody awards. Paper published by the National Center on Women and Family Law, Inc.

Woody, J.; Colley, P.; Schlegelmilch, J.; Maginn, P.; and Balsanek, J. 1984. Child adjustment to parental stress following divorce. *Social Casework 65* (7): 405–412.

Zeiss, A.; Zeiss, R.; and Johnson, S. 1980. Sex differences in initiation of and adjustment to divorce. *Journal of Divorce 4* (2): 21–33.

# Index

# About the Author

Geoffrey L. Greif, assistant professor at the University of Maryland School of Social Work and Community Planning, has been specializing in men's issues in his writing and clinical practice for over ten years. He received his D.S.W. degree from the Columbia University School of Social Work. He is currently contributing editor to *The Single Parent* and serves on the international professional advisory committee of Parents Without Partners.

Contributor **Kathryn L. Wasserman** received her M.S.S. from Bryn Mawr College and is a school social worker and private practitioner in the Philadelphia area.